VOICES FROM THE MEAD

People's stories of the Kingsmead Estate

Edited By

Roger Green

Published 2005 by arima publishing

www.arimapublishing.com

ISBN 1-84549-072-X

Printed and bound in the United Kingdom

Typeset in Verdana 10/14

arima publishing
ASK House, Northgate Avenue
Bury St Edmunds, Suffolk IP32 6BB
t: (+44) 01284 700321

www.arimapublishing.com

ACKNOWLEDGEMENTS

I would like to express my thanks to the following people: the Kingsmead Estate residents past and present who agreed to be interviewed and making the project possible. The Project Steering Group members, particularly Kingsmead residents Alec Watson, and Eileen Bradbury for the hours they put in. Beth Hammond, Community Development Worker at the Kingsmead Kabin, for all her hard work in making it happen. Mark Cohoon, Chief Executive, Hackney Marsh Partnership, for his encouragement, and Esther Collins for giving up her time.

University of Hertfordshire staff Barbara Scott, and Helen Sender, from the Centre for Community Research, and Duncan Barron, Centre for Research in Primary and Community Care, for conducting interviews with residents. Sharon Curtis, Faculty of Health and Human Sciences, for transcribing the interview tapes. Dr Michael Buckenham, Head of the School of Social, Community and Health Studies, for his support for this project and other on-going community research activity on the estate.

Thank you to Elizabeth Green, and staff of Hackney Archives Department for their general help, particularly finding photographs, and permission to reproduce the following photographs of the Kingsmead Estate: Edred House, 1947, and 1950; Kingsmead Way, 1965; and Kingsmead Estate, 1970.

Resident Alex McCarren, Andy Turner, and many others for photographs of the estate. The Hackney Gazette newspaper for their continued interest in the project.

Terry Stacey and Gareth Evans, from Renaisi, the Hackney Wick SRB Partnership, for agreeing to fund the project from the Community Chest Programme.

The University of Hertfordshire's, School of Social, Community and Health Studies, and the Hackney Marsh Partnership for their financial support in getting this book published.

FOREWORD

Voices from the Mead is ultimately an optimistic book. It is an unique project which records the stories of residents of the Kingsmead Estate, an estate which has been seen by sections of the media and social commentators as one of the most 'notorious' housing estates in England.

Located in the ethnically diverse and deprived area of Hackney, East London, and only a few streets away from the wealthy terraces of Hackney's Victoria Park, the voices of its residents provides an alternative history of this much troubled estate and its community.

Its stories tell of personal and family histories, social events, tragedies, and communal life with all its ups and downs. Painful episodes of domestic violence, racism, the grinding poverty, family life, and experiences of being a victim of crime are recorded, as are happy memories of the estate's 'lost community', where friendship, neighbourliness, and looking out for each other, were commonplace.

In gathering these individual stories from long established residents, newcomers, and people who have now moved off the estate, Roger Green has captured the residents shared identity and the communities ongoing resilience and cohesiveness.

The supporting photographs provide us with a wide range of images of everyday life on the estate, and remind us that the estate has gone through a series of rebuilding and regeneration initiatives by a succession of landlords.

It deserves to be widely read not only as a significant contribution to the ever growing body of literature on community and oral history, but also as a message of hope for Britain's inner city housing estates.

Polly Toynbee
Summer 2005

AN ODE TO THE 'MEAD'

It's not the awful estate it looks from the outside
Come and look at the lawns and trees in the evening
To see the breeze rippling through the trees
To see the sun shining on the walls of the blocks opposite
To watch the sun disappear
And to listen

Not all evenings are the same
Some are very noisy
Others, the only sound that is heard is Mother Nature

Now night has come
The slight sound of the breeze is still there
Occasionally interrupted by cars, people or aeroplanes
Lights have begun to come on in the blocks opposite
But still there is that breeze
And peace

Alec Watson
Resident

CONTENTS

INTRODUCTION

"The people of Hackney Marsh turned out in thousands yesterday to cheer the King and Queen on their way to the London County Council's great new King's Mead housing estate, built like a village, with its green and trees on the marshes"
(News Chronicle, March 31st, 1939)

Built in the late 1930's for 'East Enders' affected by slum clearance in the old boroughs of Stepney and Bethnal Green, the Kingsmead Estate is situated on a seventeen acre site in the far north east corner of the London Borough of Hackney.

Compact streets of 19th Century Victorian terraced housing surround it to the west. Whilst to the east the River Lee Navigation cuts the estate off from the famous football pitches of Hackney

Marshes where David Beckham played as a youngster. In the south the estate is flanked by the busy Homerton Road and the old Lesneys factory, which used to produce matchbox toy cars. The open space, Daubeney Field, lies to the north, behind the estate's school, the Kingsmead Primary School, its youth club, the Concorde Youth Club, and the council run adventure playground.

Originally planned and built by the London County Council the estate passed to the Greater London Council (GLC) in 1964 and then to the London Borough of Hackney in 1982. Residents voted to transfer to Kingsmead Homes, a Housing Association, part of the larger Shaftesbury Housing Group, in the late 1990's.

This book has evolved from my experiences of working for a number of years on the estate. Originally I went there in 1996 to undertake a survey examining the issues around poverty and social exclusion on the estate. At the time my intention was to carry out the research in the usual academic research tradition, publish the findings, give a paper at an academic conference, and move on to the next research project. All in all some six to nine months work.

This did not happen. I quickly realised that residents I came across were suspicious of me, did not trust me, and regarded me as yet another 'outsider' come to research them and their estate and then disappear.

Based at the Kabin, a community development project, on the estate's only row of shops in Kingsmead Way, I began the slow process of becoming accepted by the residents who used the Kabin. Slowly I became involved in the groups of people who came into the Kabin's drop-in to seek welfare benefits advice, family support, or to simply have a cup of tea and a chat. Over the weeks and months I progressed to making the teas and coffees, and serving them to Kabin regulars.

As I completed my survey (Green, 1997) in listening and talking to residents over a period of some fifteen months it became apparent to me that the history of the estate, people's experiences of living there and its problems had been exclusively told by outsiders.

These outsiders had identified problems typical of an inner-city council estate in one of the poorest boroughs in London, for example, indiscriminate vandalism; a high crime rate particularly burglaries, which in the early 1990's accounted for a quarter of all recorded burglaries in Hackney; violence and drug-pushing; low incomes; high unemployment; and poor housing. The list was endless.

Reports on the conditions on the estate and the view that the behaviour of some residents threatened the moral fabric of society were compounded by journalists and television reporters, researchers from private research organisations, and writers, presenting a negative image of the estate to the outside world.

The media in particular queued up over the years to label the estate, for example, Barwick writing for the Spectator in 1991 called the estate 'a slum', and Pearce in the Guardian (1993) viewed it as 'Hackney's Terror Estate'. Whilst Duncan Campbell presenting Radio 5's Crime Desk programme in 1996 examining how the estate was turning the tide noted that it had been described as 'one of the most notorious estates in Britain'.

Despite some innovatory and courageous work by residents from the 1990's onwards through the Tenants Association, the Kingsmead Community Trust, in partnership with the London Borough of Hackney and the Police, to tackle crime and anti-social behaviour this image lingered. Even the massive £43 million social and economic regeneration programme promised by Kingsmead Homes in 1998 has failed to completely erase the memory. The term "devil's Island" coined by Murphy (1985) lingers on in some commentators minds.

The idea for this project originated over cups of tea with residents at the Kabin. Its uniqueness lies in the fact that it has recorded the personal accounts and stories of people's lives on a much maligned housing estate that have until now have largely remained ignored or on the margins. It aimed to give what Caunce (1994) has called 'an alternative bottom up perspective'. One that challenged the 'official' and public views that existed, and in doing so has produced a part history through the experiences of ordinary people, the residents.

It has offered residents the possibility of a genuine voice in their futures (Clifford, 1995) by grounding the estate's future development in a more concrete social and historical context.

As Martin (1995), and Huerta and Flemmer (2001) have noted such an oral history with its community emphasis can also be a useful tool for communities to begin to learn about their histories, to understand the complex social and economic issues which impact on their daily lives. Also to give them confidence in confronting forms of social exclusion, marginalisation and discrimination. These are issues, which the estate has experienced over a considerable number of years since the 1970's.

Similarly in highlighting the possible contribution oral history can make to successful community development, what Rivera and Erlich (1992) have called gathering "knowledge of past strategies, their strengths, and limitations", this project moved away from previous reporting of the estate that viewed it as a community solely on the basis of problems defined by others.

In capturing the past it has the potential to influence the future. Each interview is of course unique to that individual as people recall events from their experiences that are personal to them. Taken collectively such stories can help recreate an image of a community, an estate, which has a richness of memories, of celebrations, happiness, 'good times', and lessons of community activism and traditions which have a contemporary resonance.

The stories that emerged show that the importance of family and kinship ties may be an old East End cliché but they are alive and well on the estate. Support from and giving support to nearby family members is still a daily aspect of many residents' lives. Equally the role of neighbours play a vital role in the estate's social networks, and maintaining a sense of community that has a long tradition in that part of London (Cattell and Evans, 1999).

Moving onto the estate was a mixed experience for the majority of people irrespective of where they came from and the circumstances of their move. Being a newcomer was often for some a traumatic experience. The role of council housing in this process in providing decent and affordable housing for people at the bottom of the housing ladder in temporary accommodation, being homeless, in privately rented flats, and from squatting cannot be under-estimated.

The ebb and flow of community life, including its politics, are there for all to see. Community institutions such as the Tenants Association, and the Wally Foster Centre, the Concorde Youth Club, the shops, particularly Ronnies, the Golden Shoe Pub, the local churches and its vicars, such as Christchurch, and in recent years the Kabin Project have all been essential parts of people's memories and futures. So are its community activists those individual residents who over the years have and still are involved in the life of the estate for the betterment of all the residents.

The stories of being a child on the estate and the importance of play now tempered by the concerns of parents are a poignant reminder of what it is like for children and young people growing up on an inner-city housing estate. As is the trouble caused by some young people as viewed by adults, whether it be criminal activity, anti-social behaviour, or simply hanging around in groups, which has been a feature of estate life for many years. The need for more resources for young people on the estate is highlighted in many of the following stories and in doing so supports Colin Ward's assumption in his book The Child in the City (1978) that cities should be places where children and adults can live together.

The cultural and ethnic mix of the estate has changed over the years and to some extent mirrors the growth of a multi-cultural society at large, and whilst racism has been an undercurrent in this changing process often linked to being a newcomer onto the estate, there has been a shared collective identity. It could be said that the now much used term 'community cohesion' has been in practice on the estate years before becoming a New Labour 'buzzword'.

Visits to the estate by a host of dignitaries over the years, such as members of the Royal Family, television reporters and personalities, and leading politicians, have been both welcomed and seen as a temporary respite from the often 'working class toughness and violence' of daily life on the estate. A recognition maybe that the majority of the residents are ordinary, decent law abiding people just simply trying to get on with their lives in circumstances not of their own choosing.

The bleakness of most local authority council housing throughout the UK has been much commented on. The aesthetic appeal of medium rise 1930's blocks of flats of bricks and mortar in the urban landscape are very rarely considered outside of the architect's drawings. Yet the beauty of the estate at night with its shining lights and at dawn with the rising sun, its proximity to the marshes and the River Lee was for some an ephemeral experience well worth the price of the rent alone.

Residents stories of crime, drug dealing, and particularly burglary, and how that has affected individuals lives has been a constant reminder that the estate is still slowly emerging from this period of its life. Whilst there is a recognition by residents that these crime related problems do not entirely go away there is a sense that the worst has long gone.

The estate has had a succession of landlords over the years, all have been praised and heavily criticised in equal measures. Kingsmead Homes are no different. Whilst there was an acknowledgement that the estate has improved in recent years, that it is a safer place where people might chose to live, it may take some years before the legacy of Hackney Council's stewardship of the estate is completely forgotten. The concerns expressed that the gains made need to be sustained for the future formed part of individuals hopes and aspirations not only for the estate, and the community, but for themselves in 'seeing out their days on the estate'.

Being continually amazed by how much residents, both past and present, remembered, and the detail in their stories they told is a constant feature of oral history. As is people's generosity in inviting us into their homes and talking so freely about their personal and family lives. Their stories are unique, but they tell an universal story. This project has of course only scratched the surface of the rich vein of memories on the estate, whilst there is still much more to be told the message that comes across is that there us hope for the estate's future.

2. Growing up on the Estate

Christensen and O'Brien (2002) argue that children negotiate their way in urban environments, for example, where they play and what type of games they play. For children growing up on the Kingsmead Estate this holds true. Images of the estate from school children are one of adventure and fun, whilst Stuart Belony recounts happy childhood memories of friendship, play, and the occasional trouble. Jackie White's story is similar with a childhood of playing with friends at home and at school, and running errands for her mother and neighbours.

As their stories unfold Stuart's experiences changed as he moved through his teenage years to adulthood. Now as a parent the freedom he enjoyed growing up on the estate has changed to one of concern for his own children.

Jackie having lived on the estate all her life from the age of eight as a mother she now is concerned to give something back to the community.

Children from Kingsmead Primary School

"I like Kingsmead Estate because it's good"
"I think that it's good to me"
"Sometimes there's fights but it's all right"
"I think the Kingsmead Estate is a bit messy but I like the Adventure Playground"

"I like the Kingsmead Estate because it's an adventurous place"
"I think the estate has warm houses"
"Kingsmead Estate is fun and everyone plays after school"
"I love Kingsmead Estate because it is fun"
"I like Kingsmead because the shop is funky"
"Kingsmead Estate looks small but there are lots of windows and children"
"I like Kingsmead because it's an exiting place"
"The Adventure Playground is really good for me"
"I like Kingsmead Estate because there are lots of fun things to do"
"I think that Kingsmead is brilliant and when you don't have friends you could make friends. There's lots of fighting but it is brilliant and great estate"

"I think Kingsmead is a good place for people to be"
"They like to wee in the lift"

Stuart Belony

Stuart moved onto the estate when he was six years old and has lived there for over twenty years. He has fond memories as a child of growing up on the estate, of playing football in the flats, going to the adventure playground, and riding his bike. As a teenager and in later years he recalls the changes on the estate as its notoriety grew and what this meant to him, his friends and the wider community.

I remember the summers were long and hot, there used to be lots of kids playing around and we used to go down and play with them. There was always loads of children to play with, so it was good in that respect, and I had a friend, as soon as I moved into Daubeney School, he took me under his wing. The teacher said, "Look after him", so we became really good friends. I had friends pretty quickly round here.

As a kid you have got the estate with all space in between the flats to play football, there used be thirty kids playing bulldog at one time and stuff like that. This place was just full of children and you could go over the adventure playground, you could go over the fields, always plenty to do, we were never really bored.

I remember going somewhere for the day, maybe swimming or going over and playing football, because a lot of the kids liked to play football. We used to spend hours playing football and when we came back we would relax, and then after a while we would go downstairs maybe playing marbles in the drains or something. There was always a buzz around the place.

In my early teens, a few people had moved out, other people had moved in and I had got new friends, being a teenager you didn't want to hang around, you wanted to go out and do stuff. We would ride our bikes a lot more and go other places, but the best times were before my teenage years definitely. As a teenager you would meet people in different schools so they come round and then you just go off with them. So by the time I was a teenager things had changed a bit.

There is no buzz anymore. Nowhere near like it was. It was unique over here. As a kid it was always stuff to do but as you get older and like becoming a teenager and because most people wanted to move out of Kingsmead because it was a bad area. There was always trouble.

Being a lot of people around anyway, there was always conflict with one side of the block to the other. I didn't know it at the time, but someone I met who was older than me and he was a teenager at the time, he used to tell me all the problems that they had, but I didn't know what it was about.

So I would see like a lot of ethnics in there on the estate. So there would be one block that the blacks would hang around in, you would have the other block that the whites would hang around in, and apparently I didn't know this, but you had Turkish and Greek in one side, Mediterranean types. Blacks and white used to fight, but in the 1970s there was a lot more racial tension then. Then something would happen. I remember going over the park and there was a great big massive fight but it was the blacks and whites together against someone else.

I think it was Hoxton (Estate) that came down because this already had a bad reputation. So they thought they would come over and beat Kingsmead up or whatever and that was terrible. I didn't know what that was about but I saw the same people that fought against one another was fighting together against these others. It was strange.

There was a youth club at the Concorde, that was always there, but from what I remember it wasn't open that much and I don't think most of the kids took interest in it. Maybe once a year there may be a week or two when people would go there and play table tennis.

The adventure playground was amazing, because the stuff they had built over there it was really high. There was different levels, maybe four levels, and one side of the adventure park joined on to the other, and you could play everything over there and you could spend hours running all over the place. It was like a mini estate in itself. It was amazing it really was and you had ropes and you had the army sort of thing that goes all the way down and that was really high, forty feet high from the top to the bottom. You could, if you was to fall off the top where you hung off, you would fall like twenty feet, two levels, and you still wouldn't have hit the bottom. The park was a really nice place.

I think although it was a nice place for kids to grow up, I don't really think that it offered anything for grown ups where support was concerned. To talk about my family, we didn't get that at all. When we needed help I suppose was when we was younger and you had a lot of people around and you had a lot more trouble.

There was some really bad trouble and where you would think the council would really try and help people because they really needed it, nothing was getting done. The Police wouldn't walk on the beat round here, they refused to do it. As a kid I used to think all the time why don't the Police come round here? Later on I found out why, because they refused to come on the estate.

They used to have lots of fetes and that was good and sometimes some fairs, and they used to have things like a motorcycle team come over and do the stunts, all things like that. That was good.

The best things for me living on Kingsmead was definitely Kingsmead itself as a place to play for kids. There was always something to do, it was a brilliant place to grow up. I did enjoy myself, I didn't really complain, but in hindsight I can say that because I see how my kids are growing up where apart from living over here for a year or so, they haven't had that much opportunity to just let themselves go. They can't just go over to the park just like that and meet people and play.

They have got to ask "Dad can I go and do this? Can I do that?" because the way society is now I have to be concerned about that. I have to be worried about who they are going to play with, what are they getting up to. If my Mum wanted to get hold us she knew most of the time she could come to the door, shout out and if she couldn't see me someone else would say "he went over there with..........".

Most people knew one another and because living in flats you can shout and someone will hear. We would be over the park or getting up to mischief somewhere else. The only time my parents were concerned about us or me was when I came back about nine o'clock one night. I went to my friend's, Greg, and he only just lived over there.

Kingsmead is pretty notorious, or it was pretty notorious, and for good reason because things did go on. I remember being in my friend's flat one time and there was a hole in the window like a bullet hole. As kids you think, "What's that?" and we didn't know what it was.

It was some pretty bad lot that lived in Kingsmead. Sometimes the Police would come into the estate looking for someone. On one occasion, I didn't see this, I got there just after, someone had run up the stairs and the Police were in hot pursuit, so they run up the stairs after them and you have got two sides, he run up to the second floor. He can't run any further so he has jumped off the second floor on to the floor, he has got up and run. It always something like that going on. You had people getting on motorbikes, riding through the flats. There were children, little kids running around and thinking about it there wasn't accidents but it so easily could have happened. It was a bad place and the thing was this estate has carried on with that name.

A few years ago there was something in the paper about drugs being on this estate and the people they were talking about, I am older than they are. I have seen them grow up and they were like little kids and people that have moved into the estate they talk about them like they are dangerous people. I look at them and I think what are you on about? This bloke is not dangerous.

Where people talk about these people I think they are nothing like what it was. It's just ridiculous to talk about these kids selling drugs like they are some really bad people because of the name Kingsmead. So in that respect it has got a lot better. The things that happen here happen everywhere else, whereas when I was young the things that happened here didn't happen everywhere else! There was no way you could get a cab here years ago to pick up in the 70s, 80s, and all sorts of things like that.

Its one good thing about it all that the flats being done up. Now for the first time it seems like people are more proud of Kingsmead because it doesn't look like a really bad place, well it won't do when they have finished, and people are buying their places now. Then again I think it is to do with location. No matter where you buy, as long as it is in London and this is a prime spot now.

I don't think there is much of a sense of community now at all. The people that knew one another years ago they still want to know one another, but years ago you used to get mothers talking to one another across the landing. If one lived slightly over in that corner, one used to walk to the end of the balcony and they used to chat across. You don't get that no more, you don't know people in this day, you just don't know them and even people that live next door or a few doors away, you say hello but that will be it.

There were a lot of characters. Even the mothers, you used to get arguments between the mothers and the grown ups. I remember a fight between my friend's Dad and another bloke and I dunno what that was over. Fights between grown ups you used to get that. You used to get arguments all the time because they knew one another and I suppose because of the close community people wanted to show themselves as tough or I am this or that. So there was a lot of pride within themselves.

It just seemed like a close community because us black kids and white kids we all mixed together. I have always had a lot of black friends and a lot of white friends. It was close in that respect.

I think nowadays people have accepted black people in this country now. I think a lot of it's to do with the ethnics coming over from other countries like Eastern Europeans. I think it's because of what everybody is suffering under Governments really. They realise they are not getting their lot in life and they can see it's being taken away even further because you are getting other people, other countries coming in, and taking it and they are giving it to them. So I think in that respect white people and black people who are normally are laid back and not bothered but now you are getting black people turning round and saying "This isn't right. We are not getting a lot in life".

Whereas before you always had this racial thing, not in Kingsmead but outside. If a certain amount of black people or Asians move in the area they want to move out, but in Kingsmead obviously you didn't have that because people were really poor, we were all at the same level in Kingsmead.

I think people in Kingsmead were common people, one person couldn't say they were better than the next person was. Living in Kingsmead you are all under the same level and Kingsmead was a rough looking estate. There were some rough people in the estate so really one person couldn't say they were better than the other person was.

Kids would say where you from or something horrible and you say Kingsmead and sometimes you could see the tension. My friend who lived just two roads away, a good friend of mine, he didn't want to come anywhere near Kingsmead. You might as well say he was part of Kingsmead because this was the main area and he was terrified of coming to Kingsmead. I had a friend, the same friend who looked after me in school, he hated Kingsmead because of some of the people that were on it and how rough it looked. It had a really bad reputation. It wasn't just the media. People in the area in East London they knew Kingsmead.

Maybe now that Kingsmead Homes are doing up the flats and the estate from what I have heard people moved back on to

Kingsmead. They can see that it is being re-done up. Also a lot of the people now living in Kingsmead were people that lived a long way away that don't know nothing about Kingsmead. They are thinking it is just another estate or whatever. Now Kingsmead is going to look better than other estates they are only too glad to move in. That is the impression I get. I think it's just going to develop into a place like anywhere else really.

Jackie White

Jackie and her family moved onto the estate when she was eight years old. Now in her early forties she has her own children. Her mother still lives on the estate, as does one of her sisters.

I came onto Watermead House, it was three bedrooms and there was five of us. Then when my younger sister was born a while after we moved down to here. I lived there for a number of years before moving off as a tenant of my own onto another block.

My mum was a housewife; she didn't go out to work. She had six children so she had enough work. Every day that we came home from school our dinner was ready. We'd have dinner and then after that, the next thing for me would be "I'm going to go to play" and then I'd be outside and I'd be playing and that was sort of what my life consisted of, playing at school and playing at home.

We weren't allowed to wander, although kids being kids, every now and again you did but it wasn't until we got a bit older. When we first moved here I don't think we played out, it took a while before we got used to the kids and then we started playing out.

There were a lot of older people here at one time and you got used to some of them and on a Sunday morning I always had to go and get fresh bread and also the newspapers, my dad used to have his newspaper. I have to go early about eight o'clock. On the way to the shop, you'd knock on your elderly neighbour's door and you'd get their bits and pieces for them. It was good because they would give you a threepenny bit I think it was at that time or a sixpence. I enjoyed that.

As I got a bit older I was allowed to play out. Luckily for me there was a family living along the balcony that had six children as well so we always played there together as a group and they were in the same school as us and my mum knew their parents. There was another lady that had children, her best friend actually lived on the same estate that we had lived on in South London, and she came across, we knew them as well.

So we already knew a few people, and because our neighbour was known by both of the families, it was like a little family community there already. We played together until I got a bit older and branched off to play with other children.

Mum did a lot of her shopping around here. She didn't always come over here herself that much, it was mainly me, "Oh Jackie, I need a loaf of bread", or "Go and get some potatoes for tomorrow".

The weekly shopping was done down Chatsworth Road but then as I got older into my teens, I remember going to Ridley Road market but this was their main shop and Spar's just up the hill.

She stills live here. She's got dementia. My mum's the sort of person that wherever her family is, that's where she's happy at. If we were to move then she'd move with us. I don't even think she'd think about well do I want to go, do you know what I mean, if that's what everybody wanted to do then she would happily go along with it. One of my sisters, she's my mum's main carer, she lives with my mum in the family home.

My dad had a stroke in 1983 and we were given a transfer to a lower ground floor flat and just as the transfer actually came through, my dad then had another stroke and died but then we were still moved anyway to the ground floor.

There was no real racism on the estate. The estate was predominantly white. As time went on, one or two other black families came, they were dotted around the estate sort of thing until we got into our teens and that's when there was quite a few black families on this estate but before that not many at all.

We knew of it because like at that time as well when I was that age, there was the Concorde Youth Centre and there was lots of activities going on and lots of dances and things like that. There were dances where people from off the estate were coming along and I remember an incident where the white kids on the estate used to use the Concorde, soon there were problems a few fights broke out. But it didn't really affect me. It didn't sink in as being a problem, do you know what I mean? You got the comments, "Oh you black so and so" but I didn't take it personally because the majority of the people that you knew on this estate, they were fine. So I didn't really experience racism.

Most flats were occupied. In those days I don't think you even had squatters so I think they would have all been legal people.

There's always been old people its just varied and it is today it's the same. Its now very multi-cultural, in a way though it seems to be predominantly overseas residents rather than indigenous white people, that's what it seems like but whether or not that's a true reflection I don't know but it seems like that.

The white families and the black families, a lot of them have moved off the estate, like there was a period of time when there were lots of problems and families were over-crowded, and some of the flats were damp and managed to get a transfer.

I don't know how long it's been but for a number of years now, most people that have been taking up the tenancy it seems they're black Africans and Turkish and there weren't that many Asians. At one point there were a few Asians but there's not been a high number of Asians, there's only been a few, that's what it seems like but maybe it's because they keep themselves to themselves as well so you don't really see them.

In my mum's bit I think there's only three white people now, not in her block, but in her little section. There's about thirty something flats there and the rest of them are all from Africa.

When you're young and you're a child you would move around the estate, you'd know who lives where, you'd go and knock for your friends and you'd see their neighbours. As an adult now you go to the bus stop, you go to work, you come back in, you close your door and you only see the people that are directly opposite you or the flats that you walk by.

In the past people were on the balconies and they would be having a cigarette or they'd be just on the balcony chatting to their neighbours and watching the children play downstairs so you got to see people. People would be popping into each other's houses because you didn't used to lock the doors, you'd just go into people's houses and things like that, nowadays people are locking themselves in.

A few years before the flats got sorted out, there was like a lot of people had metal caging over their windows and their doors. Some people had it at the end of their balcony plus on their door but one lady had one on the end at the entrance to the balcony. She had a gate on her door and then she would still lock her front door and that's how frightened she was and how insecure she felt. So it's bought this culture where people didn't want to talk to this person and they'd lock the door and that was it. I think a bit of it is still there because although people will smile and say "Hello" to you and whatever, nobody says, "Would you like to come in for a cup of tea?" or anything. They don't even want to spend too much time talking to you on the balcony, it's just "Oh, hi" and then they're gone, they don't want to become involved.

It could just be the change in society but then there are blocks where people still maintain good relationships so I really don't know.

At one point there were a group of teenagers going round causing havoc on the estate, even going as far as breaking into properties with people in them and taking what they wanted and really roughing people up. Hackney Council put a stop to that by evicting some of the families. That was a landmark case I think. Hackney Council was one of the first London councils to actually take parents to court and evict the families.

After I had my daughter, after about a year I tried to get a flat on the estate. Just before that there were people on this estate being transferred under what they called the 'Sons and Daughters Scheme', so anyone that was a tenant with teenage children and was overcrowded could ask for a flat for their child.

Unfortunately when it came to my turn it was "I'm afraid we no longer do that policy".

It was GLC then. I had to apply to Hackney Council and none of them seemed to be able to help. Off I went off to see my MP. Because we were overcrowded and I had a child. At the time I think he was a Councillor so I went off and saw him and he wrote to them on my behalf, both councils, GLC and Hackney Borough and then a little while later the GLC said they've reconsidered and they are willing to give me a property on the estate.

As soon as I signed on the dotted line, Hackney Council said they were willing to give me a flat but by that time I'd already signed for the Kingsmead so I just went with the GLC.

I didn't want to stay on the Kingsmead because by that time a lot of the families were moving off the estate and Kingsmead was now becoming an estate where people associated it with crime, poverty and all those bits and pieces, it was like a deprived estate.

At that time a lot of people were coming onto the system from overseas and I wouldn't say they were unduly dirty or whatever but when we moved onto the estate in the beginning there used to be a cleaner that cleaned the estate. She'd clean the stairs and the balconies and things like that and a lot of the people, the tenants themselves, would clean their own little area and they would take it in turns to do the stairs as well so although she was there to do those bits and pieces, they would do it too.

Now if you didn't know that then you wouldn't do it. Some of the people that came from overseas leaving their rubbish where they shouldn't have left it, expecting the cleaner to just take it downstairs. So I didn't particularly want to come on this estate at that time but that was my only option so I just took it. So I stayed there for a number of years with my daughter until there was problems with that flat.

The last straw for me was one of my neighbours above me, had a slow leak under her bath where she couldn't see it. Each morning I'd be going to work, my kids would be in the bath and she'd get there just before me and at the time I wasn't really thinking, it's only now that I look back and I realise what happened. She'd be coming out when they would be in the bath and as she lets out her bath water, it starts dripping through the ceiling and it starts dripping on my kids and as much as I complained it went on for ages. At the time she had a lot of stress and thought I was harassing her.

So I went off to see someone at the Citizens Advice and I told him I'm fed up with it because there was all these other little problems as well. So then they put me to a solicitor in Mare Street and he started writing to the council to see if they could sort out the problem.

So I then moved back down to my end. There were a lot of the older tenants still there, the area was kept clean and you felt safe and secure because the neighbours would look out for each other and knew everything that was going on the estate in their vicinity, do you know what I mean?

Watermead House was a much nicer environment. My children used to go outside to play so it was a lot easier for me and my mum was below me on the second floor, I'd pop into my mum's house on the way up, get a cup of tea, stay with her for a few hours and then go upstairs. It was really good.

I went back to work on and off. I then took up a number of courses at the Adult Education Institute and that went on for a couple of years. The last one was a media course, photography and communication course, because I had an interest from early on then of working within the community and I wanted to maybe write a little magazine or work in some sort of community organisation.

So I took that in the hope that it would help me to help the people on the estate. I had two children, two rooms and unless there was medical grounds, domestic violence or racial abuse you couldn't get a transfer.

I knew I'd be on this estate for a long time so I thought well let me do something for my community and my kids, so I went off and I done that. I came to work at the Kabin as an Outreach Worker and then the title got changed to Careers Advisor, which I didn't like because I didn't think I had enough experience to be a Careers Advisor. Now I'm an Information Advice and Guidance Worker. I've been fortunate enough to go for my NVQ in Career Guidance, which I've got. So I'm quite happy to be called an Information Advice and Guidance Worker.

3. Life on the Estate

This following stories give a vivid impression of daily life on the estate; the problems associated with criminal activity and general anti-social behaviour; the ebb and flow of community spirit; the reality of living in an ever changing multi-cultural community; the personal stories; and the hopes for the future of the estate as it moves away from its previous notoriety.

How people came to move onto the estate from an assortment of homeless hostels, privately rented flats, squats, and the Greater London Councils role in providing them with 'council accommodation' often away from a location they knew is worthy of a separate book. These personal memories for people of putting their new home together and being new to a growing community of housing refugees reminds us of contemporary stories of refugees and asylum seekers coming to the UK.

The community spirit which manifests itself in the importance of being a good neighbour, of helping each other, and looking out for each other is a common theme. It portrays a picture of people 'being in it together' irrespective of race or faith but with the evils of racism and prejudice never far away.

The parade of shops on the estate have played an important part in the community life, particularly Ronnies, which became the gathering point, the community village green, where people shopped and chatted. The chippie has and still does provide low cost meals during the day and evening for residents, whilst the Chemist and the other shops which have come and gone over the years are still retained in people's memories as an essential part of what the community is.

The Golden Shoe Pub with its live music was a favourite watering hole for many of the tenants and along with the tenant's own 'social club' and later the Wally Foster Community Centre they provided the estate with community focal points at weekends.

The estate has seen some difficult times such as the once high level of crime, particularly burglaries, the civil action taken by the authorities to move residents off the estate and the murder of Jason Swift by a paedophile ring in one of the flats. The latter has left a dark shadow over the estate. It is reluctantly acknowledged in some of the resident's stories but still remains hidden away as one of the estates most darkest secrets.

The stock transfer of the estate from the London Borough of Hackney to Kingsmead Homes Housing Association in the late 1990's and its subsequent refurbishment with residents in situ is well documented. For many residents this was a miserable experience to go through but one they had to endure for the promise of improved accommodation, repairs undertaken, and the general upgrade of the immediate community environment. For those residents who had experienced the days of the Greater London Council (GLC) it was the hope of a return to a better managed estate whilst for others it was simply to get rid of the council.

However residents hopes for the future and the gains made since the transfer are tempered with concerns that the levels of vandalism, crime and anti-social behaviour the estate endured for many years are not allowed to again return. What comes across in these following stories are that the estate has physically improved, people are generally positive, and the community has the strength and will to move on.

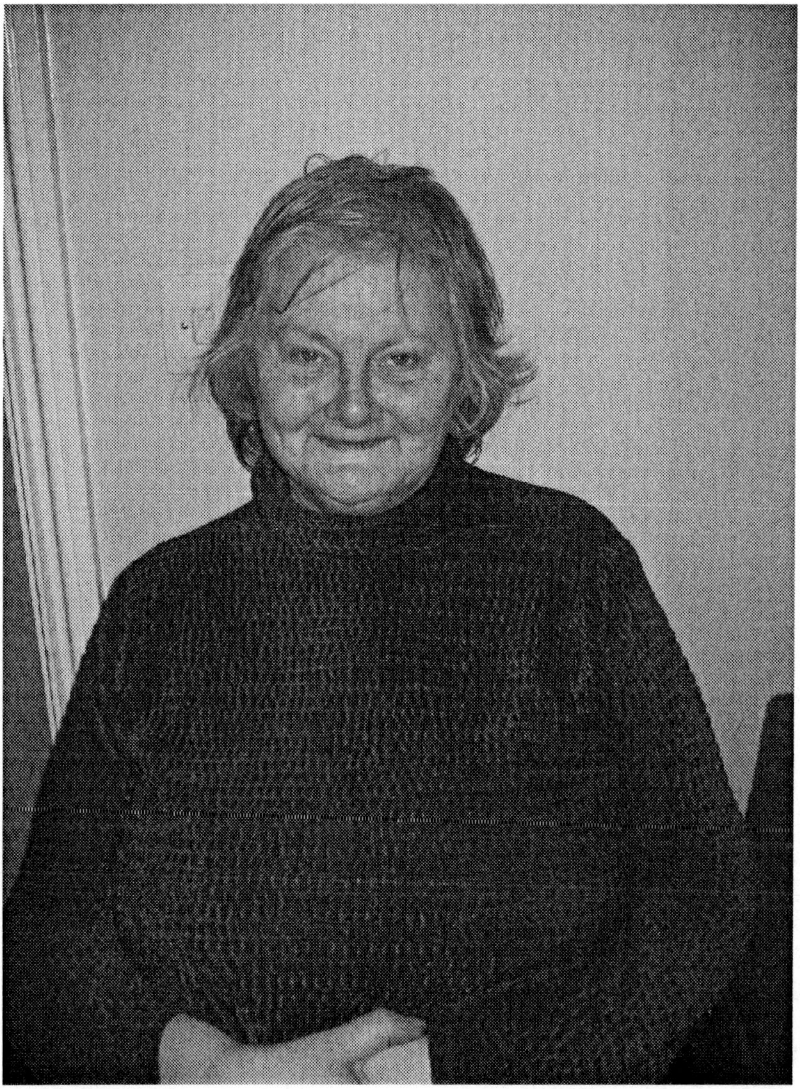

Eileen Bradbury

Eileen moved onto the estate in 1986 when the landlord was the London Borough of Hackney. She lives with her husband Dennis in a ground floor flat.
Originally from Derby, she was homeless and first lived in a squat then a hotel in West London before being housed on the estate.
During the time she has lived on the estate Eileen has been a keen supporter and user of local projects and groups.

When we moved in things had to be done like gas, and electricity seen to. My son-in-law he helped me move a few bits and bobs so that we had got somewhere to sleep on, something to have meals, things like that. We applied to the DSS for grants to buy certain things and they come through later, basic things such as cooker, crockery, and curtains. In 2000 we moved to a ground floor flat because of me having back problems, spinal arthritis, and Dennis having heart trouble.

The estate was rough because people were so much into crime, drugs and things. Like the weekend we came back after my wedding at my daughter's and someone had thrown themselves from the balcony opposite. A couple abused their child and they were prosecuted because they killed him. Lots of things like that have happened since I have lived here and they are the ones that stay strongly in my memory.

When I first moved here my son-in-law come down and stayed with us one time and we went up to the Golden Shoe Pub there for a drink. We also went up there for a drink the night that we got married. A friend in Derby she came down to be my maid of honour at my wedding and my eldest granddaughter was the little bridesmaid. We went there and had a drink and that after everything was all over and done with.

It was quite a good pub at that time but it deteriorated a bit after a while because the wrong kind of people got involved in there and then towards the end when it got caught on fire it had got squatters in there because there was no landlord or anything. I suppose somebody whoever it was who were squatting were hard up for somewhere to live. They do things because they are desperate.

I used to be on the Club Committee until I took ill the end of 1996, I had a breakdown. I was briefly on the Tenants Association when Brian Powell was in charge, I did go on it for a few months and that but it was like being piggy in the middle or the meat in the sandwich as you might say. I have been on the Wally Foster committee ever since it first come into existence. I can't exactly remember when but I would roughly say somewhere between '92 and '93 because I think it was just before the Kabin opened the end of November '93 because I remember that.

One time Chris Akabusi was up the Concorde, I don't know what for, it probably might have been to do with youth and sport because he was a runner. Prince Philip has been down, whether it was anything particularly to do because of the youth and his Duke of Edinburgh Scheme I don't know for sure, and Gaby Roslin came to do interviews here regarding BBC's Children in Need.

The other year William Hague come to open the things (artwork) on the wall at the back of Alfred House which children did. He come to the Kabin because I have seen photographs.

The shops have changed. The big shop used to be a greengrocer's shop and a newsagent. At the Kabin, the old Kabin part was the neighbourhood office for the Council. The chip shop that has always been there and the chemist right at the end has always been there. It was a white gentleman when we first moved here but he died and the people who owned the mini mart near the café on the opposite side of the road they took it over. The sister took over the chemist here and they have another one up the hill.

It's much improved the estate to what it was because the flats have all been refurbished. They have had new windows in, new stronger front doors, the front has been sort of put separated from the rest of the courtyard by little railings or whatever people would call them, and you have got your own gate.

The bay windows on the ground floor flats have been made into two windows instead of three and a door has been put in. They have sort of put fences between each house, which has meant that I have got a great big garden with a tree in it. The only bad thing about that is it takes a lot of the daylight away so we are using electricity when we shouldn't be using. Although because I am very environmentally minded I don't like the idea of the tree being cut back!

They have now fenced the back off behind Alfred House completely so that people can't take that short cut. They have refurbished the forecourts with different bricks and things from what they had before and put in bollards in certain places to stop cars parking where they don't want them to park. Adding lifts to the estate as well which is quite good for people who are in difficulty with health or crippled or got babies where they have got to have a pram or pushchair.

You do get repairs done and that, but I haven't had a great deal that has had to be done. Something happened once, someone from up above must have put something down which had done a blockage and caused my toilet to overflow all into my hallway, bathroom and that ruined the carpet there.

It's beginning to look a lot better now to what it was. There is still quite a way to go because they have got all the grassy areas to do and the courtyards of the places that are still being renovated. But hopefully they are hoping by the end of the summer this year they might be finished the regeneration and the rest of it by Christmas. Whether that will happen I don't know because I mean they are supposed to be finished by this year or they can get a penalty clause. But they were given a little bit extra time because at the beginning they were disrupted by the Council objecting to this and objecting to that.

If people begin to appreciate what they have done for them and what their surroundings are going to be like it should be a little more harmonious perhaps. I know some residents were trying to get people to vote against the estate being taken over. One has just recently been permanently moved from one flat to the other that has been done up and they are absolutely over the moon about it, so I have seen a change there!

I am quite hopeful just as it is now. Being able to rent the flat, enjoy life in there and try and harmonise the best I can with the people round and about me, just keeping myself to myself, not making trouble like. I have never been one for doing that, I mean I have had people up above me and down below me in both flats make a lot of noise but to me it doesn't make any difference as long as I am not being told I am causing the grief. Where I am is the best part of the estate, it's quiet.

Marjorie Clark

Marjorie Clark is in her early eighties and came to the UK from Canada in 1965. She has had some good neighbours over the years since she moved onto the estate in 1972 with her two children. Despite the estate's past Marjorie is hopeful for its future.

I knew Kingsmead had a terrible name at the time but I was so desperate to get my own place, I moved in here. There were lots of problem families on it and things like that. Lots of kids that were getting into trouble.

It was just me and the two children. They were about twelve and thirteen. They went to South Hackney School. They are now forty one and forty two. I had to watch what they were doing all the time because he, my son, sometimes got in with the wrong gang and that. It's so different now you wouldn't believe it. It took a long time to get like it is now. There was lots of thieving going on.

They had done the flat all up when I moved in and that was ok. I didn't really mix with a lot of people because everybody tends to just keep yourself to yourself and you will be all right. All I knew was two or three nice neighbours that lived on the same balcony as me, that's all I knew, I didn't know hardly anybody else on the estate really. But now I seem to know half the people who live on here or they all speak to me anyway.

When I first moved in here I was ashamed to tell anybody I lived here. Maybe it was just me. Several times I had to tell people where I lived, I'd get that look, "You don't live in that place do you?" So that was the reputation it had. I knew it was a bit rough but I was so desperate to get out of where I was living that I just took the first flat they offered me. I came up and looked at it, it was all nicely done and everything. I haven't been sorry I took it really because I'am not one that likes to move all the time and it was my own place, I didn't have anybody telling me what to do. Its no joke living over somebody that every time your child makes a noise or something they come up and scream at you. That is what I had for quite a while.

I had some really nice neighbours on the left hand side of me, but his father died and he got a house in Fulham, the whole family moved to Fulham and they were such good people. They gave me their gate and put it up for me. I hated to lose my gate but they said when they were doing these flats "If you want to keep your gate you have got to keep it inside your flat all the time". They wouldn't be responsible for putting it back on so I just got rid of it. I liked the gate because in the summertime you could lock your gate and keep your front door open wide and get the air. You can't do that now.

Hackney Council never did a lot. They come and service your central heating and things like that. The only thing I have got to say good about Hackney Council is that we never had all these problems with Housing Benefit and Council Tax Benefit since these people (Kingsmead Homes) took it over, it's so complicated. You fill out your papers every year and whoever is living with you and you have to tell them, but you sent them off and it is done in a few minutes, but here it is so complicated it drives you mental. These people can't seem to do it although they keep changing it.

The shops have changed over the years. There was only the grocer's shop. His name was Dennis, I can't remember his last name, and he ran it for years and then he sold it. I think it has been changed over twice really. The fish and chip shop is still there and the chemist, that is all there was before the Kabin came.

The pub at the end of the road I have been in there, it was horrible. I am not really a pub goer. Actually my father-in-law he was a publican because he is dead now but years ago he tried to buy that pub! I don't really habit pubs. It wasn't the pub it was the people who went in there! Keep coming home drunk at night. It's much better the pub isn't there any more really.

The ITV cameras were up once, what for I don't know. I remember seeing John Stapleton standing in the yard one day reporting something. There were those murders that went on here? I never even knew that was going on until one day the Police going round asking people, going in their houses and asking people if they knew anything about it. I never knew it was happening. If I had known that was happening I would have been worried about my son being around playing. A terrible thing this Jason Swift murder. That is one thing that gave Kingsmead a worse name.

It's quite okay living on the estate now especially since the Kabin came. I used to go in there a lot in the morning but I don't go out so much now. There is always somebody to help you if you need it like people from the Kabin or people from the office (Kingsmead Homes) that help you.

You don't hear so much noise as you used to years ago. There was always somebody out in the yard having a row and screaming and shouting. You don't get that now of course there is nothing but workmen around now. I think it's a much more peaceful place.

I have always had good neighbours mostly. I have got neighbours on the left hand side of me at Templemead House there, a coloured couple they are very nice. If I leave rubbish outside my door or anything he always takes it down for me when he goes to work. Some people you get living next door to you don't even speak to you. I have got another neighbour he is an Australian bloke, I have known him for years, and he does me favours. If I want anything he will get it for me. I have always been quite lucky with my neighbours.

I don't know what is going to happen in the future but I think it's going to be really nice when it is all finished. I have grumbled about it, all the inconveniences but you know where my friend lives in Fairmead House, they have done all the yards and everything and put all the fences around, it is quite nice over there.

Dawn Esmer

Dawn is a single parent who was born on the estate and is part of a large extended family that have lived on the estate for a number of years. She spent some years living in Edmonton, North London, before moving back

I have been here nearly ten months, but I was born here in Ashmead House. I left when I was about six months, my mum's property was too small because there was ten of us. We come from a great big family.

My mum still lives here but I lost my dad in January. That's the only reason I moved back here, because my dad was so sick, otherwise I wouldn't have come here. I did try years ago to get back here but I didn't.

I was living here in the eighties as well, I shared a flat with my cousin. It was his tenancy but I shared with him. It was all right back in the eighties and that generation then, I know a lot of them from back then, but the young children this day and age, personally I wouldn't want my kids to be brought up like that. Because they are swearing and God knows what else and outside my mine do swear, I can't deny that, but they don't do that in front of me, they have got a lot of respect.

Before I lived in Edmonton, North London. I was there eight years then came back. It's totally different up there. I could let my kids go out and play and not worry about it, here they are not allowed out.

I did an exchange. But when I come here I didn't realise how small this flat was going to be once my kids were here with their clothes. I mean their clothes take up most of the room. Most of my furniture is still up there. I have left a lot of stuff up there because it was too big to come up here. The woman is still holding it for me but because I am going to move into a house then I will go and get it.

I have always been back to see my mum, I have never left my mum and dad never, even when they was little I used to dump myself on their doorstep for a few weeks here and there. I have always run back to them.

They have done the flats up nice, some of them are really nice. My mum's one is beautiful since they have done it all up and that bad name they had in the eighties is slowly drifting off the estate, so that is a good thing.

I do go over the Kabin there and have a little natter with them, the girls, but I don't put myself out to involve myself with people round here. I have got a few friends from school and all that. Apart from that, no I don't put myself out to make friends.

I go to Asda or Tesco for shopping. I do prefer Asda actually. I don't like the cheap shop here, the people are nice but their food I don't like. I prefer to go down the Square.

My children go out if they are with adults or I am always at the balcony or at the window, I can see them and make sure they are not in trouble. I am not saying my kids are innocent, but they don't run round with guns and all that.

Because my brother got shot, my brother nearly went blind for it and my Dad nearly done a ten year stretch over it, so I wouldn't personally let my children run round like that. If the mothers, and the fathers as well, had a bit more control over their kids it wouldn't be as bad as it is because if you look around, especially in the evening times, you have got little groups of kids. I didn't come here for my kids to get beaten up or for my washing to be nicked, or my baby's prams.

I am a single parent so they do get what they want most of the time. I used to have loads of toys outside, quad bikes, cars and bikes and all that but these kids round here thought they would help themselves to some of it. They think I can keep going back to replace it and I can't, and what annoyed me more, not so much the toys and that, they nicked two of his bikes.

He didn't have them that long, one he didn't even have five minutes, the other one not even a year and my baby's pram that annoyed me because it was beautiful. She doesn't like the cold, she has got a thing about the cold, the rain, snow, and she just will not go out in it. So I had this big pram thinking if I keep her warm in that pram I can get about and do what I gotta do, and no they nicked it with the bag on it.

Personally I want to get a bomb and blow it all up with the little riff raffs on it. I would have knocked the whole lot down if I was in charge of all the management. I would have re-homed everybody stripped it all down and built from scratch, then it would have cleaned Kingsmead straight up. Those riff raffs, I would have kicked them out and those you got on well with I would have brought them all back.

I reckon they should have more play area for the kids. The greens at the back of the flats in between the gardens and all that, I reckon they should have swings or roundabouts, little play park just for the toddlers, but round here there is none of that. Me personally I won't take my children over there. My son has been attacked over there, his arm and all that broken. My niece had her arm and leg broke the other day over there, she come off the humps and bumps and she went flying and she had to have an operation on her arm. My daughter broke her arm over there as well because there is no one really there to watch the kids. You could say send them out and they will play over the Adventure Playground and there is people to watch but they can't watch every child that is in there.

They should give the kids just somewhere where they can go because round here there is nothing for the kids, nothing at all. I think this is why we have got the problems we have got; there is nowhere for them to play in, there is nowhere for them to play football so all they can do is stand on the corners.

The people in Kingsmead Homes they don't live on the estate, they don't know exactly what goes on, on the estate. But what they have done to the flats are better than what they were I must admit. The old Kingsmead wasn't all that, but my mum personally misses the old cupboards. She lived here for years and years, she come back to her roots really. The same with my dad, he come back to his roots, and he died with his roots.

The advantage is they have got gardens. Most of the ground floors have got gardens and this is what my mum likes, because my dad had cancer, and she has got thrombosis and arthritis of the legs.

Me personally, no it's not a place for me to live and to be honest I am not used to such a small place, everything I have had has been quite large. The flats are nice. A lot of the people are all right, but it's not for me, not for my kids. If I had my way I would be gone yesterday.

Hannah Fletcher

Hannah Fletcher moved onto the estate in 1984 from a women's refuge. A regular at her local church she has been actively involved in the Kabin Project since its inception some ten years ago. She proudly recalls the times she met with Princess Anne and when the Duke of Edinburgh visited the youth club on the estate.

I used to come on here before I lived here because I had a lot of friends on here so I used to be always over partying in the years gone by. We used to party a lot over here. I came here from domestic violence because I have got friends on here. I thought it would be better to be near friends than to go far away where I didn't know anybody so I got rehoused here.

When I went to the Council with the women's refuge and I asked to come on Kingsmead they looked at me and laughed and said "Are you sure you want to go on Kingsmead because most people want to get off, not want to come on". In those days it wasn't very nice on here. I said yes because I knew the place and I felt comfortable in it so I would be all right.

When I first came on here to be honest I didn't spend a lot of time on here. I used to go out mostly all day, I used to be with the women's refuge. So for the first five years I didn't do much on here at all. I was with the refuge a lot. But then when I left there and I was on here all day it was a different thing, I had to start trying to sort things out. The only place to go really was the Golden Shoe Pub. That is where we used to go, as there has never been much on here. The Shoe was the main thing for us. Years ago we used to spend weekends in there because there used to be live groups and everything, and people used to come over for a drink. There was some really nice people who owned it and we used to have a good time over there, but then it came out of their hands and somebody took over it over it started going wrong. But now it's knocked down.

Around about the time I came back was the time when the paedophiles came, when Jason Swift was murdered on here. There was Police asking questions, so for quite some time it was not very nice on here. Some of the families got moved off. So there was a bit of thing at the time about who you can trust and who you couldn't. Everybody was worried where their kids was and it did make a lot of difference on the estate at the time because the kids were frightened to go to the parks, they would go with a grown up for some few years. It was really quite a bad time on here.

This was when it was Hackney Council because when I came on the GLC was already abolished. By then Hackney Council were getting a bit better with us and it was funny because then we went for a change of landlord. A lot of people now think its just as bad now as the Council because when the Council started getting things a bit more better with us, Kingsmead Homes took over. I don't think they were very good Hackney Council.

When I first came here you had a very old chemist and it was still in the old shop fittings that they used to have. We used to have this guy with the fruit and veg and then we used to have a paper shop like a bit of an old fashioned thing and then a grocery shop that never hardly had anything. It was a bit more stocked but as time went on it was unstocked. In fact I remember times I used to come up here with my friend and she would say let us stop and get some biscuits or something and there was not a biscuit in the shop.

We used to have the Council Offices, which is now the Kabin Project, which's where we used to go when we used to want anything. Some years ago it was a butcher's shop because when they were doing all the shop fittings there was a butcher's thing there and Advance Laundry. When the Kabin took down a sign they had a sign on one of the sides and it had got the Advance Laundry Services, well I remember my ex-husband used to work for the Advance Laundry Service years ago.

I can't remember definitely how long the chip shop has been there, but for quite a while because before Pablo owned it there used to be a guy there, Steve, before that and I remember him from some time ago. So quite a little way back I can remember the chip shop being there.

The Tenants Association when I first come on here it used to be run by different people and then it got run down, then it was taken over and then it wasn't too bad, then it was a non-goer again. The Tenants Association took on tasks like planting, and on some ground floors they made brick square things to put flowers in. I used to have one out there and I used to have tomatoes growing in it, and I used to have flowers but now they have took it out. They did that and they put different plants in different places. So they took up a few tasks, the TA.

I never got involved in the Tenants Association at all because I never really felt that I wanted to be in anything. When I first came here I didn't have anything to do with it at all and then some people that run it I knew, but I never really went to meetings. I didn't join the TA as such. I had got bad health by then. So the Tenants Association yes, there was, but there is not now.

The greatest improvement ever come on here was the Kabin because I belong to the Church and Phil Stone (Reverend) said that we need something on here that we can really help the people. We said lovely and we sat down and we discussed about it and then it sort of went on for a little while and then luckily it was started.

I named the Kabin when Phil Stone said we are going to have a competition to see who names it. I said the Kabin with a K because I know there was a Kabin on the television, the old western thing, they all go in the cabin and they all sit there with the log fires and they all sit there. The Kabin to me is a drink and a place.

When the Kabin was first opened it was just this little one shop and it was so small it wouldn't really hold anybody, so then it started to get crowded and we had to come out there and go into a flat. We used the Tenants Association flat. They let us use it for Kids Stuff, so on a Friday we used to have all the rails in there so we run it from there and then we used to go and sit over and do all our drop-ins and our open houses. We used to go to a flat in

Runnymede House and use that. It was just a flat, a two bedroom flat, but we made it home by the time the Kabin was there. We had some good times over there, it was really all right until the Kabin was opened and then the Kabin branched out and we had two things, still not enough, we want a building somewhere else.

I think the Kabin has made a lot of difference and there are still a lot of differences needed on here. We still need clubs. We have got the Over 50's club which we go to which is nice. We used to have Bingo down at the Wally Foster on a Thursday but because the person who run it is too ill to do it nobody would stand in, we have missed out on that as well. So we need some clubs.

The Church has always been in the Wally Foster, but I used to go down there sometimes Thursday night for the Bingo. I could have started the Monday afternoon one because they have got the over 60s but I haven't been down there. We need some more places to go. We need something we can do. We are short of activities on here. All ages, not just old and young, all ages, we need something going for us.

I met with Princess Anne because the Kabin were doing something about crime. Crime was bad on the estate, crime was bad all over the place, so what they did they thought if we could be safe the Kabin gave us personal alarms, the one that you hold and press. I met Princess Anne at the Town Hall, with all different groups about this.

I have met with the Duke of Edinburgh, I have actually spoke to him. He was visiting down at the Concorde and we went down to see him and he asked me where I lived. That time I lived right near where it was so I pointed up and said that is where I live and he looked and was trying to see. He couldn't see much, but he was very nice. They have probably had some other people on here because I know the Kingsmead Trust had different people down here. So I have met the Duke of Edinburgh, and Princess Anne, which is very nice, I was very honoured.

The estate was taken over by Kingsmead Homes to regenerate it, which was the whole thing of coming over. But they are going through this really bad change, so it's very stressful. Myself if I go over there most of the time I do get things sorted out so they are usually all right with me.

Kingsmead Homes should do more to clamp out a lot of the trouble. They are told practically every day of the week whose children, who is doing what and at the end of the day they may think they are doing something. But at the end of the day to the tenants on here nothing is being done and until they address that we are not going to anywhere.

It could go well, but to how it looks now, if Kingsmead don't take positive action on what is going on to the estate and bringing in people that can make a difference we are going to go nowhere. We are going to have these lifts, we are going to have these nice little gardens. Until everything is sorted out we are not going to go nowhere. We have got the building but we are not going to go nowhere.

A lot of people have said to me it is really nice what they are doing on Kingsmead, but how long is it going to stay like that. Most estates are getting done up anyway. But a lot of people are saying that Kingsmead are getting more funding than what they are getting like on other estates, and they are waiting over so many years, we have got it, but because we never got nothing anyway, that is why Kingsmead got it.

A lot of people are impressed but think that it is getting done, but how long is it going to stay like that? It is down to us really. They have done it but what will happen to it is another story. Where will it go because we are not going to get that much money again, and we are never going to have what we have had done now again, not in my life. It would be a shame just to see it come down again.

Jenny Kelly

Jenny Kelly and her family have lived on the estate for eleven years. She was living in temporary accommodation in Wood Green before moving onto the estate. She works as a volunteer at the Kidstuff Clothing Project in the Kabin. Her son competes in Irish dancing contests.

When I came to visit my flat that they offered at the estate I didn't take a lot of it in. It was all burnt out cars, burnt out flats, but I had to accept it because if I didn't I would have made myself homeless. You get one choice and you have to take it because we had a young kid and we couldn't have refused it. I didn't really want to take it but, as I said, I had to.

William was two when we came to live here. I cried every night. Coming from Wood Green, we had a house there and garden and come to live on the estate where you had to had a security gate on your door and your window, it was terrible. I cried for months and months in the end, I didn't want to come out.

But after a couple of years you get used to it. It grew on you. It's a thing where you had to, you couldn't say well I am going to hop it and go somewhere else. Where else would you go? So we have to. We came to love it in the end. My neighbours were all right. We had really nice neighbours and we have still got the same neighbour next door to us.

The landlord has changed and we have got a lift where we never had. We have double glazing windows which we never had, and the forecourt is done better.

The tenants have changed, the atmosphere has changed because sometimes you come out and loads of boys in front of the walkway and there is always a big gang of them and you are being intimidated by them, you don't want to come out.

You always find them on the balconies smoking or having their girlfriends there or having a wee on the stairwell. The lifts are always breaking down. The intercom system is always breaking down. You think they were put there for security but it's not, because people that live on the estate let these kids in anyway. They got friends there and there is not much you can say about it. On Monday when we went to put shopping in to bring it up it stank of wee. I never use the lift unless I have my shopping.

When Ronny had the greengrocer's shop we used to have loads of fresh foods, fruits were always fresh. Ronny used to have everything. They don't have fresh food now. Their fruits are not fresh. It's totally different. Ronny used to get all sort of continental fruits and veg as well, but they cater for their own Turkish group because you go in there it is mostly Turkish bits you find.

Even before I lived here I knew his (Ronnie's) aunt, she used to work at Bethnal Green. She had a stall down Bethnal Green so when I moved from Wood Green I came here and we were talking one day and Ronny said it was his auntie. So I knew the family.

I don't trust the kids around here. I have seen a lot of things go on with other kids being bullied and being intimidated. William doesn't use the Concorde Youth Centre because he is always out

Mondays, Wednesdays, and Thursdays, and on most weekends we are not around. He doesn't have friends on the estate.

He is not allowed out to play because I wouldn't like William to be like the rest of the kids, smoking and swear at people so he is not allowed out unless we are with him.

When I first came to live here I had really good neighbours and then my neighbours on one side moved out and then new people came in and from the time they moved in we have been having trouble for three and a half years. Loud music every night, they sleep all day and play their music all night and when you go and complain nobody wants to help you.

So we put up with it for three and a half years until they were evicted for non-payment of rent. From since then we have been living in peace! It has been like heaven. Nobody interferes with nobody. Everybody that lives here knows everybody now and most of the people around where I live on either side they do shift work. The one next door to me is a nurse and the one that used to be downstairs was a nurse as well. As everybody knows that everybody is out working so they try to be very quiet.

We got moved when they (Kingsmead Homes) were doing the flat up, for nearly eight months. We moved out in June and they said by the time of the end of July we would be back but we weren't until November. We were moved out for a long time.

It was terrible. You were moving into the same block along the same balcony so you moved out yes and it was a good thing because you didn't have to put up with all the work going on, but you still get the same noise, and the noise was terrible because they were still working on the building so my husband couldn't sleep. They used to have a portakabin or whatever they called it, that is where he used to go and he couldn't sleep there either because there was deliveries being done all the time.

I am involved in Kids Stuff (Kabin Project) for about six years now. Kids Stuff is a charity that we get the clothes donated from different people and different outlets and we sell those clothes to people who can't afford to go into the major shops and buy clothes for their kids. The money that we raise we take kids out on trips. I do voluntary work in the shop.

Not a lot of people on the estate use the shop, it's mostly people out of the estate. People on the estate think they are too high up to come and buy second-hand clothes, but I buy second-hand clothes from the shop, I am not too proud of it. I think sometimes we get some really nice stuff and I can buy an outfit for about £2.50 and go out to a disco in it!

We get a good response on the trips. The feedback on all the trips have been really good. I think it should be for the estate because it's really for the estate we work. Don't matter the people from the estate don't buy, we cater for them as well when the trips come.

There are more bad things than good things living here because for instance my kid can't go out and play because the fear of being bullied or something. That is one bad thing. But the estate is looking much better than it was before. It encourages people to come and live whereas before people didn't want to come and live on the estate. As soon as they hear Kingsmead, "Oh no, we are not going there".

In a way it has improved a bit, you have got your new kitchen, your new toilet, your new sink, all modernised, but you look at it in the long run, it is the same estate you are living on. So you hadn't really changed in a way.

It would be better if we get soundproofing and get rid of all the bad people on the estate, the people who cause all the trouble, the teenage kids. It's the kids that make it worse because the parents can't be responsible for them. 11 or 12 o'clock at night they are still out playing. I think people should take responsibility for their kid at that age anyway, but they don't, they can't be bothered.

We need a play area for kids. There is nothing here for the kids to go out and play. No equipment or play area. You have got the Adventure Playground but there is not much going on in the Adventure either. At weekends the kids are running wild because there is nothing to occupy them. Kids like doing their own stuff. You should have activities to cater for everybody, but there is not much. I think they should have play areas.

I don't know about the future. My husband doesn't work here, he works in Ealing and we put in for the last two years for a transfer nearer to work because he spends about four hours a day travelling because he uses public transport. All the Housing Association has to do is to nominate him and we are still waiting for him to be nominated.

Carol Maynard

Originally from Bath, Carol moved onto the estate from rented accommodation in Finsbury Park over twenty five years ago. Married with two children she has lived in the same flat. Carol sings in the local Church of England choir.

I came here with my sister and a friend and we worked in catering, we were in paid accommodation to start with and then the council gave us this. I think they were just trying to fill up the flats because nobody wanted them down here.

When I told some friends of mine that I'd got a flat on Kingsmead Estate, the first thing they said was if you only went outside if you wanted to get mugged, which wasn't very encouraging. We knew nothing about the estate.

We just wanted a flat, we didn't care young and twenty you've got the world at your feet, I could have tackled the whole world then.

Quite a few of my block moved in when I moved in, within a year or so. I think they'd just decorated it before we moved in, and the heating and everything.

One thing I thought was brilliant about here was it only takes two minutes to get to Leyton Station or Bethnal Green Station depending which way you wanted to go.

We never knew our neighbours as such, usually it was single women with children, so their hours were totally different to ours. Because when you're working in catering, it's busiest at the weekends, so you'd have the weekdays off, we never had time to meet anybody.

When I got married everything totally changed. I got married in Bath. We went home regularly to my parents. I think that may be what breaks everything up for me is we used to go away every holiday and weekends.

So I wasn't stuck here because I know a lot of people do feel that, but we never had that. I think that probably makes a difference or made a difference to me.

I come from a big family and we're all big so I've never had a fear of anybody I suppose and we were all taught how to fight when we were young.

I love London. I like the diversity of it all, the different people and you know where you stand. Growing up as a black person in a small city I was the only black one in my school, you know all the underhand racism, there's nothing that anybody can tell me that I haven't seen or experienced. To come here and if somebody didn't like you and they'd say it in your face, it was just so nice.

Honestly, you just know where you stand with people and for me that was it, I didn't care where I was that's what I wanted and that was enough for me. I think this is why I love Hackney so much, it's so multi-cultural.

There's so many different things and you can go anywhere in Hackney and find all your nice bars and things. Because I do a lot of singing as well, classical, I used to travel round quite a lot so I've travelled out of London a lot.

I joined the local choir, the Hackney Singers and it's quite a vibrant set of people there because I've always liked classical music anyway, that's what my teacher at school got me into.

There's a lot of different people living here. We've had some Turkish come in, in fact there's everybody around me, but a lot of Turkish people are left. We went through the stage when a lot of the refugees came from Turkey, the 'country people' they were called.

There were a lot them, I think most of them have moved off and then it's like whenever there's a country in trouble we get refugees from there. You get a surplus of them which I think offends a lot of people because there's people on waiting lists for years and then the refugees come in and got the flats. So although the Kingsmead is supposed to be the dustbin (they used to say) people were still quite upset when everybody else got the flats.

I used to complain at church I had nowhere to go during the day after nursery apart from going home, so I thought it would be nice for somewhere to drop into. So the idea for the Kabin came up, although it took five years to get off the ground that's where it sort of came from.

There are lots of things that have opened up, the Tenants Association have opened lots of things but a year or so later or not even that, and they've closed down.

The trouble at the Concorde is the other children, because there's still a rough element, and my son sometimes has a fast temper and is always in fights. My daughter just stopped going which a lot of the girls did. I've always felt they should have more team stuff going and the Concorde was the perfect place.

I remember the pub, oh yeah. I remember going in there years ago. Then it got to the state when only druggies used to go in there or if you were selling drugs and then it changed hands. It used to change hands quite a lot but it was just always there.

They changed the estate over from the council to Kingsmead Homes. Well they couldn't have been any worse than the council were we decided it was just that we were all so fed up with the council and everything.

We felt we weren't going anywhere. The Housing Office was terrible, you just couldn't get any joy from them at all. I think because when my husband went and started university, they had to have student loans and things and his wage just disappeared and he started going through the benefits system and all that. That was a real eye-opener for me, having to fill out a form for things. It was sort of demoralising and then you'd keep speaking to people on the end of the phone and you'd think well I know why people get fed up.

During the refurbishment they moved me to one of the inner blocks and that was another eye-opener. For the first time I felt like I lived on an estate because I was right in the middle and every window you looked out of, someone was looking in on you. I've never experienced that before. That I found very, very weird, I didn't like that at all, I felt it was like living in a box.

It's been a bit of a fiasco, the refurbishment. Some of what they've done is nice but it's just the quality of the work, a lot of it is rubbish. If they'd put a bit of extra effort here and there it would have made all the difference, but you just got the general impression from the workmen we're here doing you a favour, be thankful for what you get.

I've got all the right colours and everything that I wanted, although I've had to go over and check everything. There were some real stupid mistakes made which they corrected quite quickly. It definitely wasn't a woman who designed the kitchen, I know that.

The worst thing here I think is the lack of something for the children to do the lack of facilities for them. Well the facilities are there, like the Concorde, I know the Concorde's out of action at the moment, they're working on it now.

We don't have the gun problem down here like they have up in Tottenham and Clapton, just up the road, and break-in wise, we did go through a phase about ten years ago where we had a lot of break-ins but I think everybody knew who it was, and the council knew and banned these certain boys off the estate, that made quite a difference.

Since Kingsmead Homes have taken over I think that's made a lot of people feel a lot better about themselves and about where they live, it's much, much better now, it's much nicer. On my section of the block, all upstairs and downstairs, most have bought their flats.

I think now all we have to do is get the children's things, we've got to get the clubs up and running and I think it will be fine.

Although people do complain about Kingsmead Homes I just think it's normal. Hackney Council would never have done this, we would have been up to our ears by now, probably the building falling down around us. In my block there was a lot of damp and I could not ever have seen the council doing this, not in a million years, they'd never have the money anyway with all the corruption going on, that's not been very helpful at all. It annoys me because Hackney has such a potential, the potential down here is fantastic.

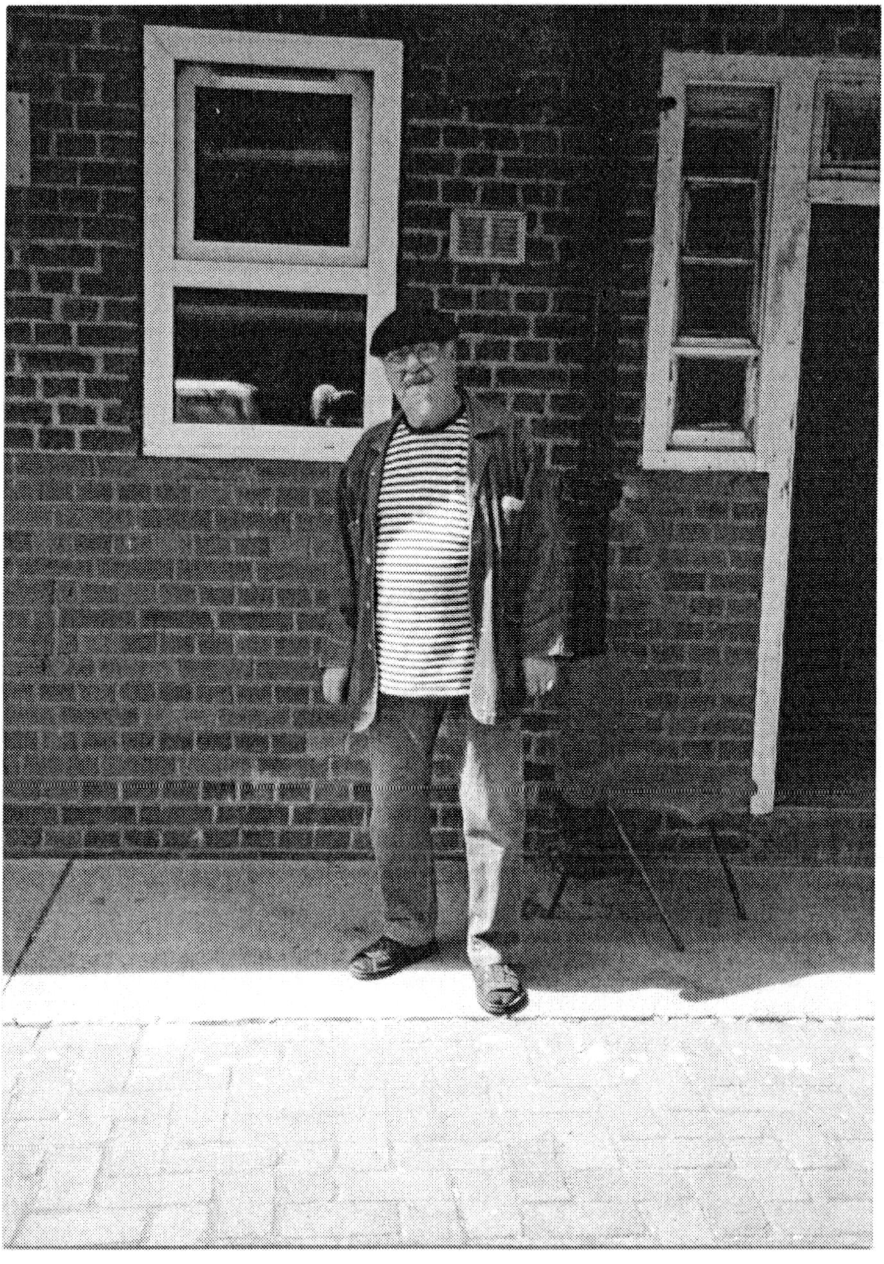

Jimmy Nash

Jimmy decided working down the pit as a miner/electrician was not for him and he left Scotland at the age of 17 and headed south. He later played for Bournemouth F.C. as a professional footballer and then non-league.

Jimmy has been a supporter of minority causes all his life. A member and supporter of the Claimants Union he was also heavily involved in the squatting movement in London in the 1970s. When he came onto the estate in 1977 he supported ex-mental health patients who had been rehoused there. He admits to being anti-establishment and is proud of his anarchist politics. Jimmy lives with Kathy whom he met when he was squatting.

When I came here there were plenty of empty flats, I'd say hundreds. Nobody wanted to live here. There were loads of riots and things, yeah it was bad, it was bad. It was a dumping ground like. It was bad, really bad. There was fucking racists and bullies on the estate. It was linked to drugs.

Kathy, me, and the baby, Moira, was eleven days old when we came here. When we got here, we came in the December and we had no windows, no hot water and we were left all over Christmas. We had nothing, no hot water and then the porter said do you want to buy a heater? I was going to fucking kill him man, yeah. It was broken windows all boarded up, the place was in a state. We had a boiler, an electric boiler someone lent us.

Yeah somebody lent us an electric boiler. Somebody lent that yeah for the baby, so that we could have hot water to wash the baby and that. Oh yeah it was hard and it was a cold winter, Moira was only eleven days old. Anyway we'd no beds, all we had was mattresses on the floor.

Kathy went into the Social and they wouldn't give her any money so they said they'd send her a giro, so Kathy freaked out so she got sectioned (Mental Health Act, 1959). They took her to the general hospital and I had to take Moira up to give her a fucking drink and that was because of the Social. I used to take her up every four hours to get breast milk, yes. This is real, this is true.

I used to get some stick when I was pushing the baby in the pushchair, this white guy pushing this black baby. I'd fucking had it, there was fisticuffs. After that I was accepted.

I was in the Tenants Association, it was a good TA. Yeah, and then two of the committee became Lord Mayors (Mayor of Hackney). They were on the TA, and then they joined the Labour Party and the next thing man it's Mayor. We took up repairs and everything because people were interested in it. There was money went missing when other people got in and a new computer system, and there wasn't even a fucking inquiry. People wasn't interested. When they seen people becoming Councillors or running away.

We ran a football team, under fourteen, me and a friend did that and the first year in the league we won the League Cup. A guy sponsored us, he was a boxing champion, he sponsored us and then we got too good for our League so we joined the Essex League, that's when my trouble started, the racism did start there.

One game we played a team from Braintree or somewhere and there was this guy on the line I think, he was shouting. His son, one of the boys got ordered off, he must have told him he couldn't take anymore. When we went to Walthamstow in front of the Football Association in Walthamstow, I said, "Well this was this Scottish guy who was doing all the shouting" so the guy said to me "How do you know he's a Scot?" I said, "Well I'm a Scot".

We were a good side, I mean really we were a good side man, you know what I mean? Then when the team died a death, the parents wanted to know why, the parents of the kids living on the estate. "Oh what's happened to the football?" and then you say, "Well why didn't you help us?" They didn't want to, they weren't interested but when things went bad it was "Oh my son looked forward to it".

We used to train a couple of nights a week and it was "Oh now it's gone" but the parents as I say again they weren't interested, they just wanted to be getting out of that place. The kids missed it, they missed it. I remember once when we had a game, it was a Sunday, and there was a market there over in the East End by the Docks.

We were going in and before the game started there was a fucking battle. Yeah man it was bad and this is fourteen year old kids man, and the man that was causing it, I'm not talking about a youth, a man, you know what I mean?

I used to play with the kids, yeah I used to play with the kids and my own, I'd always play goalie man and the kids used to come and used to come when ours used to play at home. The kids used to look forward to it, you know what I mean man? Yeah it was great, it was good.

Always had a dog, yeah always, a couple of years ago it died. I used to go with the dog all around. It was great by the river, yeah that was great, that was great man. We used to go over in the twilight and we used to see the foxes and I used to take the kids and all the rabbits used to come out then, the kids loved it.

People say "Oh I see your estate's getting done up", I say "Yeah, but it's still got a bad name". I blame the Council because when people were asked if they wanted Social Security to pay for their rent, you know what I mean or they wanted to get cash, a lot of the ones wanted cash and then they had a bad load of fucking debts. I blame Hackney Council but what gets me is that people when they run into problems man, they complain but it's too late.

So Kingsmead Homes has tried to pick up the bad payers the money that was owed to Hackney Council but the ones that thought they were okay and now they're not so they run for help. They think they're fucking shrewd, do you know what I mean man? It's always the same innit?

People don't talk, they don't talk to one another, they're not neighbours, they're acquaintances. There's no community spirit, there's nothing. You see when you walk through, there is nothing. I mean there's sick people on this estate, there's me, I can't walk, I can't get out but there's other people, nobody does fuck all for you.

Why don't people talk to one another, that's the only way the place is going to change if people get to know one another and there's no fucking dealers.

Me and the neighbours, Irish family, we're the only people that are here for years and years. I know them, they're the longest here, all the others are newcomer's man.

I know the kids, you see the kids going to school, I talk to them.

It seems a bit safer than it was, yeah. I mean there was a lot of break-ins but now they can't break in, they can break in up a stairwell, you know what I mean because of the five locks, you can't catch that door. But there's still little cliques running about in here, you know what I mean?

They used to sit over there. They tell you they've got nowhere to go. I mean the kid's playground over there, you can take your kids over there for a swing but there's no swings, the seats, they've set fire to them and then they tell you they've nowhere to go and yet the Concorde done everything for them and got all the equipment in for them so why they can't go there instead of setting fire to it.

It's bad news, the parents must know who they are, do you know what I mean? The parents must know what they're up to but the parents are just "Oh no, my boy wouldn't do that".

It's got quieter, it's a bit better, yeah but people don't talk to you much. They're all into their own thing now. There is no community they don't even talk to you man. I mean I talk, if someone wants to say hello to me, I talk to them, and some of them I've known for years and years. It's just a place to live, that's all it is, it's only a place to live.

The future I don't know. I haven't got a clue. People want a place to live but to me it's only a flat, it's a roof over my head, I get nothing off the Kingsmead, I owe Kingsmead fuck all. I was here before Kingsmead Homes, I lived through it all. I haven't got any debts, I don't owe any fucking money, what do I get off the

Kingsmead? I'm seventy years of age, I'm sick, really sick, diabetic and cancer, Cathy's sick, what do I get? I get fuck all, we just get our pension off the state.

Postscript: Jimmy died in December 2004 shortly after this interview. Residents and friends from the estate attended his funeral.

Norah O'Reilly

Originally from Ireland Nora moved onto Kingsmead in 1969 as a widow with two young children aged three and five. Her children grew up on the estate and are now both married and have moved out to Essex. Nora still likes living on the estate and considers there is a good community spirit despite all the changes she has seen.

I came from Ireland, my husband was dead, and I had two children. I wasn't three years in the country and in a private flat so I couldn't get a place in Newham. So they asked if I would move to Greater London, it was the GLC, and I said I would move wherever it was near enough for my children to go to school in Forest Gate.

Believe you and me I have walked places to try to get a flat, especially when you are a widow with two girls, they didn't want to know. If it was a woman with two or three dogs on my own I would get a flat, but because I had two children I couldn't. Some people prefer dogs to children. So I moved to Kingsmead. I liked it here, people were nice and quiet and it was very clean.

At the time you couldn't even drop a piece of paper on the floor. Our porter lived next door to me, his name was Andy, and if he saw anyone dropping paper he would come over and tell them off. He was out in that courtyard every morning at seven o'clock and you could eat your dinner off the place it was so clean. There was a porter in every block and they all worked very hard, up to nine o'clock in the evening you could get anyone to do anything for you.

They were doing the cleaning and they would come in and put in bulbs for you and everything. They were very good and then it changed, it changed an awful lot, for the worst unfortunately. Some of the porters retired, Andy retired because he was pension age, he moved up to Trowbridge Estate I think. He often called to see me after he moved but unfortunately he passed away.

The other porters moved on to different places and new ones came in which weren't as good. The place was neglected. Rubbish was left thrown around different places and it was a shambles. It was a different Kingsmead from about three years from the time I came into it.

The neighbours were all very helpful, very good. I can say all my neighbours in both flats I was in. I lived in Rivermead House first and I moved here in March 1977 from Rivermead because I had a bad accident and I wasn't able to go up and down the stairs, so they gave me a ground floor flat and I am very happy in this flat ever since. I have no trouble with neighbours, with anybody, and all my neighbours are very good.

The GLC really looked after us but Hackney Borough neglected Kingsmead because they didn't care who they put into it. So long as they were able to get money out of the people they couldn't care less who they put into Kingsmead and the place became a shambles. But since Kingsmead Homes have taken it over it has improved a lot, but we can see it going downhill again.

One thing, you can't get a window cleaner in Kingsmead, never could. When I came here first there was a window cleaner and he came every Wednesday once a fortnight. I never used to see the man because I was at work but my neighbour next door used to pay him and I used to pay her.

Then I used to have a young fellow, he lived across in Edgar House, his name was Paul and he used to clean my windows and my did he clean them, they were wonderful. They were like a mirror, but he left Kingsmead Estate as well, I don't know where he moved to but I lost a friend and a good window cleaner.

I had a garden outside at the time and he used to look after my garden as well for me. I used to have lovely flowers and that and a little wall all the way round. Of the evening the youngsters used to gather round my door and they used to be sitting on the little wall round the garden talking. They were very quiet. They were a nice crowd of boys and they have all left Kingsmead now, including my own daughters.

At the back of the shops there was a swimming pool for children up to nine, and there was little huts, and the ladies used to sit in the huts and make tea. You could go down and have a cup of tea at any time. The ladies looked after them. They were very nice ladies as well. They were retired and they used to look after the children down there through the day and the children were quite safe there, but there was no one over nine allowed in there.

Carmel and Una (daughters) didn't mix with the children round here because they had their own friends in Forest Gate, and they used to go there because they were nine and eleven when I came here and they had their own friends. Carmel used to go round with Sandra Kelly, she has left Kingsmead now. They were two little devils but they were very good at the same time. Sandra was a lovely girl. I think she moved on to Edmonton or some place like that. Herself and Carmel were the same age and they went about a lot together. Una was very reserved, she didn't bother with anybody. She came home and did her work and she had her friends at Forest Gate and they used to come round here to see her and she used to go to see them.

My girls were quite happy here because they had their friends outside Kingsmead. They were all the time in Forest Gate. They stayed around here very little. Then they left school, they got their jobs and now they have left home and one is living in Wickford and one is living in Westcliff-on-Sea. Una is in Westcliff-on-Sea for twenty four years now. She moved straight down there when she got engaged and they got married.

There was no Community Centre down on Kingsmead, we had the Kingsmead Tenants Association and they ran a bar at the back of the shops, it was a building at the back. We used to run a pub there at night, for a whole lot of the Kingsmead crowd and then we applied to get the pub moved down to the Wally Foster when it was open, and we got that, and we used it on a Friday and Saturday night, we used to have loads of people there. We worked blooming hard, very hard, what we did when we were at the back of the shops. That used to be crowded to the door Friday and Saturday night. All Kingsmead people used to go in there. The women with their children, their grandchildren, and that is where I got to know other people there because the mothers and the children, their daughters, the whole lot. It was a great family place. You couldn't get room there on a Friday night and we used to work so hard, but it paid off. We were happy. We didn't get any money for it, but we were very happy doing it and we were a good crowd, we worked very well together.

Kingsmead Tenants Association got that pub going we had lots of parties there, lots of charity events and everything. We used to have jumble sales.

I was on the Tenants Association for a good many years with Ken Hanson, Mrs Brown, she is dead now, she was Mrs Gray at the time, she died a few weeks ago. Ken Hanson and Claude, I forget his second name now, he lived in Templemead House, he was the Chairperson. There was about nine or ten of us who ran the Tenants Association for a long time, but then again it fell through. I don't know who is running the Tenants Association now.

We used to have trips out for the children during the summer. Whatever profits we made we used to have a trip to the seaside for the children every year. We took them to different places, Blackpool, Sittingbourne, Bournemouth and different places. We always had a Christmas party and an Easter party for them, all run by whatever profits from the pub.

Unfortunately a lot of these people have passed away now. I think there is only Ken Hanson and me left of that lot. Mrs Allen died, Mrs Dyer died and Margery, she was only a very young mum and she died a couple of months ago. We were a very happy crowd. But then again when the elderly ones have gone and there is only a few left, you don't meet as often. I miss them a lot. We were never people going in and out to people's flats but we had a good community spirit between us.

Sid (Mecoy) took over the TA. (Over 50's club) and I joined that quite a few years ago. We go there every Thursday with our Bingo and a cup of tea and a chat. I look forward to going down there on Thursday afternoons. We have outings as well. On the whole I must say Kingsmead is a good place to live.

I don't go out as much as I used to, I am old lady now. The only thing we really want is to have the estate clean. Its a shame to let it go down the pan like it used to, but its people who live in here, they don't care where they throw their rubbish. You can't educate some people. Some people are making an effort to try to keep their place better but then there is another one that won't.

Builders don't help either because builders leave a lot of rubbish hanging around. They don't come and tidy up after them like they used to, they just leave the rubbish for some other mug to pick up.

People think that Kingsmead is the old Kingsmead years ago when there was a lot of crime and everything, but I don't think it is like that any more. There is crime, there is drugs, but then where isn't there crime and drugs? It did get a very bad name and unfortunately that bad name has stuck but the odd one here and there has caused that. But speaking for Kingsmead I can't say anything about it, I can only praise it, but then you could talk to some other one and they will give you a different story, but that is my story.

When I came in here first people said you won't stay long, but I proved that I am here now over thirty years. It's near the hospital, near the schools, near everything, near the church. That is what I like and there is a good community spirit. I am going to stop here. I am not moving. I've everything I want, comfortable flat, garden back and front, my flowers and I am quite happy. My family comes and visits me and I can go away when I like. It's a pity people don't appreciate what they have got. They will when it's gone and once it goes it goes. Now they are doing every effort to do the gardens and I hope the people will appreciate it. I wouldn't move out of Kingsmead.

Joseph Paul

Joseph is West Indian and remembers when the estate was predominately white when he came in 1973. He recalls the good times in the 'social club' on the estate and the nearby Golden Shoe pub, the lack of racial prejudice, and the community spirit. The future for young people concerns him.

I have been here for thirty four years. It was 1973 I came on this estate, things have changed quite a lot. There was about six West Indian people. Ben, Peter, Rodney, and Stella and Grace, and myself. Everybody was white people. All the white people some of them died or moved out. We are coming to only one generation now, West Indian, African all of them. It was a horrible estate but now it is coming back better. The white people were living a better life. We were close, everybody is one.

When I first moved on the estate the estate was more cleaner. I lived on the end flat, my nice flat, everybody washed the landing. They do it by turn. That time was the GLC, then Hackney Council and it changed. With the GLC we got a better service.

One thing we don't have is central heating. Every five years they decorate your flat for you. Every five years the GLC come and do the flat for you. Since Hackney Council took over in 1980 everything changed. Your flat they don't care about it. Hackney Council make the flat more down than the GLC.

The pub, the Golden Shoe, they closed it. Since I came on this estate that was the pub I used, very nice pub. When we come here that was our pub. All of them that was our pub. When we went into the pub, no prejudice. I could sit down there. When the pub finished we had nowhere to go, we had to go out somewhere, but that pub used to be very handy for the estate.

That fellow Ken Hanson used to have a club behind the fish and chip shop, it used to be our club. Every Friday and Saturday if you had a small baby you could come in there and play dominoes, we had a drink, the drink was cheap.

When they left you had to go in the Wally Foster. Ken left. All of them left Kingsmead. Since then we seem to have no life.

They should have something to help the people on the estate. Say I was getting married, or my sister get married, or my daughter. I live here it is ok and I go in to ask the hall and we give a small donation, but if I want that hall in the Wally Foster or the Concorde, I have pay £70 an hour. How can I pay £70 an hour? Wally Foster is £40 an hour.

It can't be expensive for us, we live there. It could be expensive for people outside. If I have a funeral where will you have to do it? Outside the funeral everybody to have a cup of tea or have a drink, you would have to pay.

They used to have Bingo every Monday and Thursday, but the Bingo caller was too old, so Thursday you leave it, only Monday. No only the Thursday one I used to go and that is it. To me they should have something, organise different on the estate.

Jack Dunning Estate they have got a hall there and they play Bingo there for ages. Since I came in the 1960's Temple Road is where I used to live. Since the GLC they have got a hall there, only here there is nothing for us and we get more population here.

Yes it has changed, but the human being has changed. It has changed for the different colours. When I came here white people lived here and I got a better life with them. If coloured people come in, people from other nations, you have force them to make friends with you. I say, "Hello how are you?" You could say I am a stranger.

I could leave my door open. I go could shopping and leave my door open. The people would watch until you came back. I can't do that now.

In the old days when I come, the young boys very bad. Now it should be better because they Police the place better. All the young boys I meet they have no respect to me. They used to respect the elders but not now.

The good things being modernised, we have got better living conditions. We are better inside, could be better outside. The worst conditions are the young ones, the behaving. They are breaking up the lifts before it is even completed which is a shame, all that money. I have actually gone to put bars back up on my windows because I am feeling very unsafe again. The young boys, you can't say a thing. When you are coming up the stairs they don't live here.

They regenerated the buildings, now they need a regeneration programme for the people that live on here, that are coming on here, how to live. How to look after it, how to behave. Other people coming on to the estate making it bad again. We need better policing. The Police need to have a better hand on here as well as everybody should take on. The Police need to have a different outlook otherwise we are going nowhere again.

If you see something, go into the office and report it but it don't make no difference. That is why those young boys grow up and they don't like me. I say I know your mother, I know where you live. They spend too much money

You can certainly improve for the money, we pay the rent, we pay the costs and the mothers see those kids do it. Before they modernised that place all them kids playing there they dig the bricks they put on the end and the mothers look at them like that, they let their kids do it.

Now we have got it easy and we should appreciate it. Their friends come in and their friends mash it up, they never tell their friends don't do that because Mum lives there and we live there. It up to the Government to know what to do, it is not us.

Sometimes I go to the fish market and go out and come in at four o'clock in the morning. The beauty of Kingsmead in the night, all the light and the colour is very nice. All the lights shining from the balcony to the middle of the yard. It looks lovely. I hope it can stay like that. The estate has got better.

Jill Phillips

Jill and her family were one of the first black families on the estate. They experienced racism in the 1960s when they moved from rented accommodation in Highbury, North London. She has brought up seven children on the estate.

We were in a house, part of a house in Highbury. I had seven children so it wasn't big enough so we put in for here (Kingsmead) and I got it. We were the first black people to move here as far as

I know and it wasn't very nice. There was a lot of prejudice when we first came. They didn't like any foreigners.

There was a family that lived above me and if you stood on the balcony they would throw things and call you all the names under the sun, like "niggers". They had a garage, but they used to mend car engines up there and the oil from the engines used to drip through. You daren't say anything because they were horrible. My friend at the end of the balcony who lived next door to them she also was with a black man and she could stick up for herself, I was a scaredy cat. The mother was quite nice but I think the boys ruled her and in the end I think they got evicted. They were holy terrors they were.

I was really happy because we had a bathroom. We had the basics. We had a coal cellar as you come in the door. Them big old fashioned dressers and that sort of thing. Then the Council done it for us just plain white which was ok.

When we first came here there was little pram sheds in the yard, they were lovely, tiny little sheds, then we used to have our own clothes line, all this yard used to be our clothes lines and nothing was ever interfered with. We used to have a rent man come round for the rent, he used to knock at the door. It was lovely with all little trees in the yard then. It was nice.

I shopped locally. We used to have a lovely greengrocers round there, it was lovely. Fresh fruit, everything was fresh and beautiful. There was Ronnie's and Dennis's, side by side and in fact I often see Dennis now. His was just a general shop, you could buy anything in his shop. The grocers, Ronnies, was next door. You know like a family-run shop where everyone knew everyone, it was lovely, everyone used to chat, in fact we used to sit and have cups of coffee round there sometimes. The shop now has been took over by people who are very pleasant.

We used to have some lovely family do's in the Shoe (pub). Ollie, the landlord was Irish. He died and his wife has got another pub opposite Victoria Park. Then another chap took it over and I don't know what happened, it went down the pan.

I used to take my Mum and Dad over there on birthdays. I am not a drinker but drank in moderation. We used to dance to music, the Irish bands used to go over there, not that I am Irish, but I loved it.

Half the estate was in there, especially Friday and Saturday. Then they started having barbecues outside and if you wanted to use the pub for any event you could use it and they charged a few quid. It got burned down, three years ago? Squatters got in and it was burned down. Actually we stood and watched it burn.

My sons used to go over to the Concord Youth Club. That was good, they used to have bands and discos and things. Then there was some trouble and that all died down and different people took over.

We used to go regular to the Tenants Association. They was really trying to do well and Lynn and Cameron they were really good trying to get things sorted on the estate but it dwindled down to nothing. They used to put notes through doors, leaflets on the dustbins, all over the courtyard, come to the meeting at seven thirty or eight o'clock whatever it was and if you are working come another time. But no one turned up in the end, it was just me and maybe one or two others so it was a waste of time but they was really trying, they were good.

You need people. In fact when people was moaning and groaning at me in the yard, I said look why don't you come to the meeting and you can say what you want to say and all what is happening and we will try and get something resolved.

I don't know why, I suppose some people worked and they were tired when they came home from work, but they could have made an effort once in a while, just to bring things together to see what we could do.

All sorts of things was being brought up. All sorts of issues. It was to do with people at the desk, up at the Housing. If you put in a request for something and they were taking their time, it was all that sort of thing going in and in the end we just go so bloody fed-up because no one was turning up.

We used to write newsletters once a month. You used to get a lot of information in that and you know like what we spoke about the meetings used to be in the papers and everybody used to get them, but people just don't bother.

Hackney Council saw the estate as a nuisance. When you used to get on the bus you would say Kingsmead Estate please and they would say what "Hell's kitchen"? It was awful. In the Hackney Gazette there used to be Court Reports. Anyone that had gone to court for anything at all there used to be a whole page and it was mainly Kingsmead Estate. They don't do it anymore though. I don't think they are allowed to give names and addresses now.

There used to be a terrific lot of break-ins. You could sit here and literally watch people kicking in doors and by the time you call the Police, the Police just take their time and they don't even bother, its like nothing to them. Then it quietened down. Its nice now other than this vandalism and a lot of them is from kids from other estates that are coming in.

I am happy here. People say why do you live on Kingsmead? I could go across the road and leave my door open, and get a paper and come back and I know my flat will be all right. I have got no fear which is silly really. The kids say to me Mum you just go out and you leave the door open sometimes eleven and twelve o'clock at night. I feel that, a silly way of thinking really, I wouldn't do anything to harm anyone so no one would do it to me, but people from another estate could come up. Mind you we have got a security door now.

I have my best friend next door. When the dustmen were on strike me and Ruth, my mate, that same one, we set fire to all the dustbins, but we had a hose ready to hose it down. We set fire to them because they were stinking and there were maggots but we didn't realise there was glass and bottles. They were on strike forever and rats coming up all over the place because of the heat and no one was emptying the dustbins. I would do it again as long as we had a hose!

There are all sorts here, every nationality. I think it's nice when you have got all these nationalities as long as they are pleasant. I have an Indian, I don't know if they are Indian or Pakistani, underneath and they are lovely, always fetching me food. So I am really happy. The chap next door is perfect. They are all lovely.

The people downstairs are Asian. Even if they cannot speak English properly they try to, they smile. Once we get to see each other regular we always say hello and have a little chat, I like a mixture. I chat to anyone, I don't mind as long as they have got a smile on their face it don't bother me!

Kingsmead Homes had a meeting last week about vandalism. I love kids, I don't care what they do, but when it comes to vandalism I won't have it. It's a shame because they did it all lovely and they are just smashing it up. It's a shame. I scream and shout at them all day.

What has annoyed all of us tenants is these cameras (CCTV) are not working. We are paying for those cameras. If they had those cameras working they could catch this vandalism. You could get up tomorrow and the glass is smashed in the lift or excrement on the stairs.

They are situated just at the back of this lift. They are working because you see it going round and round and the last time what happened was gypsies across the Marshes were stealing a lot of property, cranes, big diggers, and we phoned the Police and they said where is your security? There is nobody there. They put a camera in with no bloody film in it and go trotting off.

There is a good security guard here now down at the bottom of the grounds where those little huts are. I think he is Greek or Turkish and he is very good, he is here weekends, but the others were just sleeping all day. So this is our main problem. If the cameras were working they could catch such a lot of this vandalism. We were supposed to have a Community Policeman but I have never seen him. There is the Concord and everything over there and they could go and take a course over the Kabin but they don't want to. So they really have tried Kingsmead Homes and it would be lovely if they just didn't smash everything up.

They are supposed to be doing a lovely park in the flats at the back there, in Egbert House, that used to be a little swing park there, they are going to do a flower garden and water for the kids, a pond, its going to be very nice if they keep it like it. Since they took over the estate it has been a lot better.

The Kabin is fantastic. There is a free advice bureau. There are quite a few good things that is going on over there and then upstairs I think they do computers for the kids, they are teaching that, there is a little bank over there, the Credit Union, that is brilliant. You can put in £2 a week if you like and at the end of the year you have got £52.

I have been to the pantomime. In the evenings they take you by coach, instead of paying the full price you might pay £3, you go to Stratford Theatre and you go and watch a pantomime and they bring you back. I have been to quite a few of them. I have been days out, Southend, Brighton and places like that. The coaches are full up.

Before my husband died eleven years ago we lived here all together with the kids and as the children grew up obviously I still kept the flat. My children have bought their own houses, they have gone further up to nicer places and they boys say mum come up to where we are but I say no, I know everyone, I like it. They all live around. They are here nearly every day with the grandchildren. That is why I want to do up this flat because I have got such a big family.

I think if the vandalism stops it will be lovely. If not it will go down the pan. It has got to be coming up to forty years now I've lived here. Unless I win the Lottery I am staying.

Catherine Sullivan

Rehoused by the Greater London Council from a hostel in Paddington, West London, Catherine brought up all her eleven children, seven girls and four boys, on the estate. She worked whilst bringing up her family for twenty three years in the old Hackney Hospital giving out the tea to the patients. She is now in her eighties.

I'm from Ireland and I came to England on my own to work. I worked in a hospital at Hyde Park Corner for a few years and met my husband over here.

The children were born and I had a place in Paddington in a halfway house and that was too small so they moved us up here fifty years ago. Its four bedrooms and a living room, we wanted another room next door but they wouldn't give it to us, the GLC.

I had all the children to look after and I had to work in the Hackney Hospital up there, I worked there for twenty three years. It was a general hospital. I used to give out the tea and serve the patients and have a singsong with them. I think they are refurbishing it now. Someone said they were. It was a very good hospital.

My husband had to work on London Road. He used to work at night and I used to work at daytime and the oldest girls used to take the little ones to school.

We shopped up on the corner. When we get me wages at the end of the week my husband used to buy the clothes for the kids and I used to buy the shopping, that is how we used to manage. We managed the housework between us. The kids used to come up to meet me from work and we carried the shopping down. We had no choice.

We had very good neighbours. Nearly all white. The coloured people are very nice on here too. I think people keep to themselves, they do yes. The woman across the road comes over sometimes. If she gets a bit bored she comes over and have a chat. Three years ago, there was another lady, she died near Christmas, and she used to come down every night and have a cup of tea and cakes. She died last year from pneumonia. She was seventy four or seventy five.

I have had trouble with the people on top of me but I reported them and they have quietened down since. They kept banging the ceiling and broke the last one and this is a new lot they put in. They were banging all the time and there used to be gangs up there. All that has stopped now.

We had all new windows and they are doing the rooms out. They are doing a very good job, they are very good workers. We went over across the road to number four for a couple of months that was all right. The whole place was re-done.

At Christmas all the gang come around. We have turkey and chickens. Norah across the way, she used to do the turkeys for me and then we got the vegetables up there and the son comes around and he serves it all up.

We sit on the table and the kids will sit on the floor! We enjoyed ourselves. Then the son would come down and play the accordion and keep them all happy. One of the girls she plays the accordion. We dance around.

I used to have an association with the Church but not lately. They don't bother coming around. I used to go to Church every Sunday but as my knees are bad I can't get anywhere. The school sent the children to Church. They were very good like that. They still go to Church.

I like living on the estate and the people are very nice. I have no fault with the people at all. There is nothing bad about it really. They were very friendly. There was an old lady there I used to look after and get the shopping for her and bits and pieces whatever she wanted and the lady in the corner. The oldest girls used to go and get a bit of shopping for them. We looked after each other.

All the people say hello and that. They move new people in, but you make friends with them, you don't turn your back on them. If they come to the door for anything you just try and help them out. There is nothing more you can do!

At the moment the kids are growing up and they can do a lot of damage, banging and crashing and all that sort of stuff. They will be about 16 and they don't know what to do with themselves. If they had something to do for them it would be better. There is nothing for them. They won't spend the money. If they spent the money on the kids and give them something to do it will be all right. I think they will settle down now. All the people will settle down.

I can't get out at the moment because I have got a broken knee, my knees are playing me up, I have got acute arthritis. The daughter over there, she does a lot of bits and pieces for me. She is very good.

The doctors are over there and you order the stuff and go over and get it from the chemist. It is very good over there, will do anything for you.

The transport is just down the road there, the buses and everything but I don't because my daughter she comes up from

Witham like and she takes me around sometimes if I want to go anywhere.

I have been three or four times back to Ireland. We lost my brother, he died there last year and I have got a nephew over there and I go and see him now and again. I like Ireland but I don't think I would go back. I have been here a long time now and I have enjoyed my time.

Alec Watson

Alec has lived in the E9 area of East London all his life and for the past twenty five years on the estate. A registered disabled person he has probably attended more estate meetings in recent years than most other tenants. He is currently Vice Chair of the charity, the Hackney Marsh Partnership, which the Kabin is part of, and sits on Shaftesbury Housing Tenants Steering Group.

I have been here since 1977. The GLC were trying to fill up Athleston House and I could have had any flat I wanted provided it was one bedroom. I picked the one right at the top, right at the corner overlooking the marshes, It was a fantastic view. Still it nearly killed me it didn't have a lift.

In 1982 I changed from living in 49 Athleston which had sixty five stairs. I got asthmatic bronchitis and my doctor said unless my landlord (it had just changed then from GLC to the Borough) rehoused me either on the ground floor or the first floor, they wouldn't be responsible for my health.

I live in a first floor flat now and I asked for that flat. The Estate Officer, Barry, said "I have only got one, one bedroom on the ground floor and I want that for an old lady". I said "You give it to an old lady, I'll tell you the flat I want", and I told him, 11a Fairmead, and he said, "Is it empty?". I said yes, the previous tenant had moved.

The first day I walked in there I was disgusted. Squatters had been in and what was on the walls and the ceiling was pornographic to say the least. Minus the radiators. In October, which was rather cold, no form of heating except a two bar electric fire in the lounge and that was it. The whole place needed redecorating and the Council didn't want to know. So myself, my mate's mother and her daughter we done it between us. The bedroom we left, we done the lounge and the hall, re-papered it and decorated it.

The flat has got my dining room in my hall. I have had seven people sitting round it in. Mind you, they couldn't move once they were sat down. It's a converted wash room. If you go back far enough, talk to the old people, they say I used to stand in what is now your hall waiting for my washing to be done what is now your kitchen.

I have got what was the drying room as well as an extra bedroom. I use one as a study.

I ain't been burgled down here (current flat). I suppose I shouldn't say that. Before then five times, four times in one month. I had actually been away on holiday for a fortnight the first time and came back and it was all alright, went to work and when I came home at night I had been burgled. One day they took my bike, not out through the front door because they couldn't get it out as I was on the end of the block, I had a trap door in the ceiling in my hall. They had come through the roof, smashed the trap door, took what they wanted, including my bike, and went out the same way.

People causing most the trouble ain't on the estate anymore, they got moved off. We had a spate of burglaries and some got moved off, a family, the sons got moved off and the sons had a Court Order against them not to come within about two miles of the estate and if you did you go inside.

The Police got fed up with coming. In fact they told the bloke at Hackney Borough Council, I asked him to put in a new front door and they said no you only had one a week ago. I said it ain't my fault I got burgled.

They used to sit on the balcony wall, put their feet against the door and push their knees down and use their knees as levers and take the door off the hinges. Smash them off because that is how flimsy the doors were. It is only two bits of plywood with wood round the outside and a bit of packing in the middle. I don't worry about being burgled now I am insured.

The estate got the nickname 'Devil's Island' through a book. It was about a chap called Jimmy Murphy and his brother who at one point fought with axes on the estate.

One time a black cab wouldn't come down here. They would drop you up the top of the hill by the old Hackney Hospital but wouldn't come down here. We have had lots of break-ins.

I think it has still got a bad reputation. But I know estates in London that are worse than this and not far away as well. They think "You don't live on Kingsmead do you?" and I say "yes". I like the place. Most of my friends know what I think about this estate, I like it.

The Hackney Gazette used to publish three times a week and most people bought the Hackney Gazette because they done a Court page to see how many people on Kingsmead had been in Court. That sort of reputation for either thieving or whatever. Most of it was burglaries.

There is not that much crime. It's better now. People lose washing from hanging their washing out on the line, people might lose their pushchair, kids nick it or somebody will nick it from outside the front door, but I have not heard of any burglaries lately. You get people speeding through the estate yes, that is a sore point.

It's five years since Kingsmead Homes took over, about 1998. The estate looks a lot brighter. There is a lot more lighting. We have got trees. They have done away with flowerbeds that people had outside their front door. Now people have got a little front patio, they have got a dustbin thing where they can put their rubbish in. There used to be flowerbeds I don't think they will put them back. The Council came down and put plants in them one day but in the morning most of them had gone. People opened up their front doors and took them in as houseplants and that is the truth.

When Kingsmead Homes come in they have supposedly got CCTV cameras. They have got people looking in the offices at Kingsmead Homes. The offices are round the back and the cameras are linked to them. The cameras don't move. They have got film in them but rats run along the tunnels where the pipes are, the cables are, and bite through them so they are forever re-laying the cables.

So little things got changed, but it got to the stage the same people turn up to the meetings every time and the only time you see somebody new is when they want something. As soon as they get it you don't see them again.

I was on the Steering Committee for Kingsmead Homes, and also KRIC, which was 'Kingsmead Residents in Control'. I am now on a cleaning forum and a parking forum. I have been on it for quite a while. They had a meeting last Wednesday night, everybody on the estate had a letter informing them of the meeting and there were only two of us. There are normally three of us, nobody else.

They don't want to know. They might moan. You have got two choices, you either give everyone a diary or hope they write it down. If they want to go to a meeting they will write the date down. I have got meetings right up to November for Kingsmead Homes. Other than that put a poster up a week beforehand and other than that forget it.

They put the rent up by 1% or inflation plus 1% for five years and now that has gone. My rent has just gone up four and a half quid per week. £64.49p. But on top of that and it ain't showing on the rent is another £60 for support. But I don't pay the £60, the Government does. They brought out something last year. Officially it didn't start until 1st April this year, but they asked you to sign a bit of paper and they said we are getting something like social workers, and I said I don't like social workers, I got rid of mine as soon as I could.

It's a new scheme. It is only for those people who are on Housing Benefit. Nobody told us they were going to put £60 on the rent, my rent suddenly went up by £60 making it £120 a week.

I think it was about the first week in March this year I had a letter to say I am your social worker or your support worker, any problems. I said like what, "If you got forms to fill in" and I said if I can't fill a form in I will go in the Kabin. 'If you have got any health problems' and I said "Forget it, I will see my own doctor".

Roughly 170 people on this estate are getting support. This is provided by Kingsmead Homes.

What I can understand because I read it in the paper, it's a Government initiative. The feeling on the estate and my feeling is these support workers ain't worth a light.

I think it is going to end up as Kingsmead Homes want it. Let's say 55% of the people are going to buy their flats which is just what Kingsmead Homes want and then they ain't got to worry about repairs. Selling Council houses gives nobody a chance. There are people in the flats who have got four or five kids. Now there are not any four bedroom flats that I know of. Its a bit unfair to have a load of kids like that in a flat with Council houses round the corner that the tenants bought because all right you can get it cheaper. If you want to buy a house I think you should save up but now the situation has changed. Houses prices around here are £250,000 plus. You have got to have a good job to get something like that.

I still love the estate. I wander round here, round the building site. I suppose in some ways it has changed. They don't look as grim as the used too. The brickwork has been cleaned up and we are now getting plants in sections.

But it is still the same, there are still some people on here that are the estate's own worst enemy. The people on here will tell them, because you have throwing rubbish out and allowing the kids to do graffiti on the walls, which is a lynching if they get caught.

There's not really is a sense of community on the estate. I think people watch out for me, the people who live opposite me do. If I don't come out my flat within two days and they don't know I am away, they get worried. I look out for an elderly lady, who lives downstairs, I pop in get her a paper four or five times a week, take a prescription in, and collect her tablets. I am just one of a few people who do things for her. It gives me something to do and I hope that when I get to her age and I am still around somebody will do it for me. I suppose there is little spots. There is a big Turkish contingent on here and they seem to stick together.

I really love this place, I like the buildings, I think it's a beauty in the place. It's the buildings, the people. I like the people. I like the estate. All right you could get somebody who can't speak English but you say hello to them, and smile as you say it, they will either nod or smile back at you. They say good morning in whatever language they have got.

There is a different culture now, it's like your United Nations in here. Back in the 70's it was all people from Hackney, Tower Hamlets, Stoke Newington, the local area. Very few ethnic minorities. Might have had some yes, but now it's multi-national. When it was Hackney, Kingsmead was a dumping ground for anybody. Any tenants they wanted off of other estates came here whether they wanted to or not.

Its a colourful estate, especially when you get people in their national costume specially if they are going out on Sunday and most of them will say hello. If you say hello, I will walk past anybody and say good morning to them, most people will either say good morning back or nod.

I shall be here until I go out in a wooden box. I go away to Birmingham quite often, my mate, a vicar, is in Birmingham. I have been asked if I want to move there. People at his church have asked me when I am going to move.

I am going to North Wales in a couple of week's time, I actually get withdrawal symptoms if I am away a bit too long. I can't wait to get back. I just miss the atmosphere of the building, my flat, and the people.

Unnamed Resident

My flat is my home, for 20 years, the estate isn't. Previously I was in another flat in Hackney over on the Cassland Road. I was only in that flat for about three or four months. I shared it with somebody, and before that I lived for three months in East Finchley and the reason I lived up there was I spent about five or six years abroad and I came back and just needed somewhere to live.

A vacancy came up on this estate and I moved in. It was nearly half empty at that time, they couldn't get people to live here and my whole thing was what is the chance of a single bloke getting a three bedroom Council flat.

I have tried moving on a number of occasions. I don't like living here but I do like the flat and things are such that I couldn't move into a one bedroom flat. I have offered on a number of occasions when the Council were running it to move into a two bedroom flat, opening up a three bedroom flat on the estate for a family. I am 53 years old and I have got stuff, I have got things, I couldn't go back to living in a bedsit or anything like that. I like the flat itself, I am very comfortable with the flat, and the flat is home but not the estate no.

I think the layout of the estate is terrible. A bit like Colditz! I remember when I first saw it from over on the other side of the green I thought "my God that looks awful". Mind you on the other hand I think if the estate was a private development and the flats were sold off you would get a lot of money for them.

The reason I didn't move when I was offered was that the Council didn't seem all that interested. They knew why I wanted to move and all the rest of it and I just kept on being offered flats on worse estates than this one, the crime rate was higher. I was shown one flat and there was an internal landing and all the other flats had been broken into. The Council just didn't care which was the reason why I voted for the change of landlord from the Council to Kingsmead Trust or whatever they are called, Kingsmead Homes. It wasn't faith in Kingsmead Homes it was just complete disgust with the Council.

They promised everything and delivered nothing. I have been to residents meetings and Council meetings and "we are going to do this", and "we are going to that", and at the end of the day they did sweet FA. The money disappeared somewhere, the plans had been changed or new people were brought in. People were farmed off to some other project. Everything happened apart from what we actually wanted to happen.

We certainly wanted a crackdown on the crime and anti-social behaviour. That would be the top thing. It was grinding you down, going out and wondering if you had been broken into while you were out.

I've been burgled twice. I knew who did both of them, it was different people who did both of them and the first time I lost virtually everything of value. The second time there was very little taken because I had the precaution of when they broke in they couldn't put the lights on because I took the fuses out of the fuse box. Nothing serious was taken, there was nothing serious to take, the took an old amplifier and it was stuff like old passports with stamps from everywhere I have been in the world. I have been to most places in the world and that was sentimental value, that was all it was.

The changes that I have seen have by and large been for the better. The biggest changes have come with the new landlord. I didn't take much interest in them, I was just glad the Council were out of it, the Council were just a nightmare, they still are.

I didn't move out when the conversions were done, I wish I had but I didn't. I need the phone for every day life and work. I am very happy with the flats, the flats are lovely. They have put double glazing in and that cuts down your heating costs tremendously. I didn't like the fact they took out the fires, I like a fireplace, I think a room should have a focus. I think they hired the wrong people to do the job. The people who called themselves plumbers, who worked in my flat, it was just awful. I knew they were wrong because in fact when I was a teenager I used to work as a plumber's mate so I know some basics, you know hot water is supposed to come out of the tap with the red bit on, not the other way round!

All the windows were double glazed, all the outside walls were insulated, there was a new hot water central heating system put in and I like that, you don't have to heat up a whole tank. I know it is not much use for families and stuff like that, but to me it is just great.

There was new electric's put in. I got a much bigger kitchen. I had an old laundry room, which I am very happy with. By and large what they have done is good but there was too much cheap labour employed. People who could screw in a nail so they called themselves a carpenter. It was pretty shoddy work a lot of it, but on the other hand it is much better than what it was. The heating used to be terrifically expensive because it was metal window frames and the heat just went straight out. Now these double glazing plastic things is something I appreciate.

There is a lot more people live here now. There was a lot of empty flats when I first came here and for quite a few years that figure just got added to, there was more and more empty flats until

I would say there was at least a third empty, possibly even half of them empty.

The Council used to encourage certain people on to the estate rather than to discourage others off the estate. I thought that was a good idea and I can't for the life of me think why they got rid of it.

What I thought was if you are getting in nurses and doctors and firemen you are getting in shift workers so you have got a constant 24 hour people coming and going on the estate all the time which is a natural thing of reducing crime. There is simply more people about and they got rid of that. I knew some of the doctors and nurses that lived here.

I very rarely get on local buses because they don't go anywhere we want to go basically. If I get all the right connections I can be in Central London, Oxford Circus, in forty minutes from leaving the front door but that is out the door, on to a train, off the train, on to a tube straight there.

There are no shops round here. There isn't a bank in the High Street. There hasn't been a bank in the High Street for all my time here and I am told there was one donkey's years ago. The shops that are available you wouldn't go there to do your shopping. It is easy enough for me I can walk to Tesco's or wherever, but I think for someone who is infirm it must be a nightmare for them.

You have got a lot of open spaces right next to you, you have got the Marshes, you have got the river which runs through the Marshes and then you have got the Lea Valley Park which goes from the Thames right up to Hertford.

I can only think of no more than half a dozen people who I know live on the estate I have seen them out there walking on the Marshes or by the river. There is one person in particular on the estate, I have never seen her any further than the front door. I have never seen her across here at the shops or outside of the courtyard where she lives, I have never seen her go anywhere. I don't know how she manages the shopping, whether she does it or what, I have no idea.

One of my gripes about Kingsmead Homes is that quite some years ago now, a criminal family basically were evicted and a lot of people, me included, put our heads above the parapet. We stood up and were counted and we finally got them evicted and this new landlord let them back on and I went over and complained about it and I know loads of other people did as well and I just lost all faith in them after that. It took a lot of time and a lot of money to get rid of them and just walked back on and these people said ok. I couldn't believe it and simply lost all faith in them. That is just stupidity.

I think there is less crime than when I first came here but I think that is down to the improved security which really isn't all that much. The doors into the blocks themselves you can actually pull them open. The new doors are good. There is a lot less crime but I don't think there are any less criminals on the estate.

There is a lot more Africans here than what there used to be. They seem to be ok. I mean people from Nigeria, Gambia, and Zimbabwe. I think its as diverse as it always was, I just think there has been an increase in African people.

There is no reason in my mind why the estate shouldn't be here in two hundred and fifty years time, it's solidly built.

Diving into the realms of fantasy, if you were able to empty the estate and put better shops and better transport links, people would pay half a million to live here just because the way the flats are. Your two up two down terraces on the next street up, their about two hundred and sixty five grand they are going for, I can't imagine why round here but that is the price.

I don't know what the attraction is because apart from the Marshes and the Lea Valley Park itself which I regard as a great boon, there is nothing that is actually positive about the place. There are no cinemas nearby, the buses don't take you anywhere you want to go, it is all right for me but for an elderly and/or infirm person it is a bit of a trudge to the train station and its uphill.

If you are paying over a quarter of a million for a two up two down terrace here, what is one going to cost near the Angel in Islington or somewhere like that. It must be an incomprehensible price and there is quite a few people bought their flats.

I thought about buying my flat back in the late 80s but I didn't because I was actually brought up in Council housing. My parents did end up living in their own home but I was nearly fourteen when they did that and I think its a good thing, so I didn't buy it and since this lot has taken over I have considered it but now its out of my price range.

I like the flat, but I don't like the estate. I don't like a lot of the people on it. It's a combination of the criminal element, the aggressiveness, the rudeness. You walk out and there is just litter all over the place and people complain about that and it is the people who live here who do it.

I take the point of view you can hardly complain about your neighbours making a noise on a Friday and Saturday but when it is half past three on a Wednesday morning and they have got the stereo cranked up full blast, no. I don't want any mediation, I don't want to sit down with a moron that does that, I just want them to say you do that again and you are out and they do it again and they are out, they actually mean it.

The time I have been here I haven't made a lot of friends on the estate, but I have made a few and they are very good friends, very close. The relationship has developed over the 20 years.

If I move out of Kingsmead it means I move out of London, and I have spent most of my life in London and I am very fond of it. But no if I could work outside of London I think I would move out.

4. Past and Present: The Estate in Photographs

The Past

1945 Victory Parties

Schoolgirl 1947

Edred House Living Room 1950

Estate 1965

Kingsmead Way1965

Dustmans Strike 1970

London County Council

1980s to the 1990s

Children's Playground

Rubbish dumped

Watching people

Protection against burglars

Council building works

Forbidding estate

Regenerating the Estate. The late 1990s onwards

Building Works

Lifts being installed

The new children's playground

Front gardens

Back garden

Estate trees

5. The Community Activists

Introduction

There is a long tradition on the estate of residents 'getting involved', becoming active in the community, whether through the Tenants Association, or the myriad of other community action and self-help groups, which have come and gone over the years. The notion of the 'active citizen' or the 'community champion' now popular in New Labour Government initiatives is nothing new on the Kingsmead. Such 'unpaid heroes' as Polly Toynbee has noted in her book (Toynbee, 2003) working with and on behalf on the community is captured in the experiences of residents such as Ken Hansen, Sid and Eve Mecoy, Ron Newman, and Brian Powell.

For Ken Hansen it was the influence of his parents in Jamaica and a sense of duty that led him into working for the community, whereas for Sid and Eve Mecoy it was their eagerness to speak their mind and get people organised if they came across injustices. Being 'community minded' and the concern about the lack of facilities for children and young people on the estate first led Ron Newman to getting involved. Brian Powell has seen it as part of his civic duty to be active in his church, the community and other local organisations such as the school.

Ken Hansen

Ken Hansen lived on the estate for 10 years between 1973 and 1983. During this time he joined the Tenants Association, becoming its secretary, and was involved in a number of estate campaigns against the then landlord the Greater London Council as well as being active in a number estate initiatives for the tenants. In 1982 he became a Hackney Councillor and represented Kings Park Ward in which the estate is located.

I came to the estate, after living in Stoke Newington. As a young married man we starting to have a family and the accommodation we had was minimal. It was one bedroom, living room, and kitchen we had at the time. Shared a kitchen and bathroom. So we said we would like somewhere a little bit better or bigger. We applied to the local authority which was the Greater London Council (GLC) at the time. Kingsmead Estate was GLC property. So we applied to the GLC and then we got the accommodation here.

When we came to view the property the porter said to me we have two places that you can look at and this was on Runnymede House. He took me to the top floor of Runnymede House and I said definitely not. With our children, not up there, not on the top floor. He said we have a ground floor but he didn't think will take it and I said why? He said because it's not in a good condition. However, we went and looked at it and it was in a terrible condition. Youngsters on the estate at the time had chucked bricks and stones and also other things through the window. It was really not in a good condition. I said "I'll take it" and he was surprised that I took it. My wife cleaned it up and put it into a very lovely living home.

At the time I was working with London Underground at Neasden Depot. I transferred from Neasden to Northumberland Park on the Victoria Line, which was much nearer to home.

Working for the community

I'm always like to be involved in something or the other. I take community life to be precious and I think everybody should be involved in the community life. My mum and dad used to do so much in Jamaica, especially in the church part of it really.

I've always been involved, from the early days. I want to give my penny worth, if one thing my dad told me, "Ken, respect, show respect to people. Always have respect for people but never be afraid of anybody". I will show you respect but I am not afraid of approaching you. That's me. I have that concept all my life. I go and get involved,

Getting involved in the tenants association

There was a thriving Tenants Association (TA) on the estate. It was one of the good things that I know of when I came on the estate. I immediately started getting involved and starting to know people on the Tenants Association Committee. I attended meetings and asked my little questions and put in my little imputs. I said I would like to try and join this and they said, "please do".

So I joined up at the Tenants Association meeting. At that time the chair was Mr Jack Sheppard. He's since died now. It was a good TA. It was a mixed group of tenants, black and white.

The estate was mainly white. But there was a good number of Afro-Caribbean people on the estate and other ethnic groups, but Afro-Caribbean was the highest number of ethnic group on the estate at the time.

In those days in the 1970's the TA was on track for quite a lot of improvement on the estate. I became Secretary of the TA, late 1973 to 1983. Mr Sheppard in his wisdom thought well you know we have somebody here who thinks he can take over my mantel.

The Mead Club

One of the first things that we did, we thought must be something for the elderly. There wasn't anything going on so we started our club for the elderly, called the Mead Club, which was in a purpose built building just round the back behind the fish shop. It was for the residents on the estate, so we used to use that hall for our teas, parties, and dinners. Before that we used to have the TA meetings in Templemead House.

There wasn't anything much for the elderly people on the estate. So we started to look into the TA and see what we could do and the first thing that we thought of was something like a tea party for the elderly. We started a Bingo Club and believe me that caught on like wild fire.

We used to have good times here. But not only that we did have outings, we took younger people as well on outings and sometimes we put on a beautiful tea parties and dinners from funds raised by the TA.

I remember we have some people attending one of our dinners when they saw everything set out they said "Oh who are the caterers?" and I said "when you have finished eating I'll introduce the caterers to you". So when everybody finished eating and feel happy and glad about everything I said "Now can we have the Kingsmead Caterers please? They were all members of the TA and their families.

We started to have a bar in the club so we can generate funds. Sometimes when we run out of beer we used to go up to the Golden Shoe pub and see Mr. Oliver Ollie (landlord), Ollie we used to call him. "Ollie, we've run out of beer, can you let us have a keg of beer?" and he would give us one or two. He never takes pays for it when we sell it until we were able to do our own order from brewery. But Ollie was very kind, he and his wife was very kind to us.

When we ran the club, we had our own music system and the music system provide our entertainment for the estate. I mean for those who come to the Mead club. Later on when we did move to the Wally Foster someone broke in and stole it. It was a youth from the estate who stole it. I think in the end the Police did get it back.

I was so annoyed to hear that the Mead Club is taken away from the tenants. It really was something where the TA could have their meetings, and now it has turned to something else over there. The Mead Club was something that was provided by the tenants for the tenants on the estate is now no more. It's using for other things. I'm so annoyed about it, knowing that was a purpose built building for the tenants on the estate, especially for the elderly tenants.

If there was a campaign going now to restore it back, I would join up with the tenants on Kingsmead to make sure it happened again.

Football for young people

With the young people there was a problem because although we have the Hackney Marshes and the Mabley Green just over there, that's a play space for young people, a lot of young people seems to want to stay in the courtyards and play football. Most of the tenants wasn't very pleased about it. They used to have a go at the youngsters.

One of the turning points was, I thought well at one of our TA meetings I'm going to invite some of these youngsters there. I remember inviting about five or six to the meeting. I said, "look our TA meeting is tomorrow night I would like a few of you to come to answer a few questions. Why do you play football in the courtyard annoying other people?" they didn't want to come, however they came. I did something that I shouldn't have done, I should have informed the meeting. But if I had informed them proposing I want to have young people there, members may object, so I just said to them "Come to the meeting" and they came. I said to the committee "Well, these are some of the young people who play the football and who you have been criticising. We will now have a discussion about the playing of football in the courtyard".

The TA members were expressing their concerns, what these youngsters were saying were when we kick the ball some of the older people telling us off. So at the end I decided one of the things that I think I will do is to try and organise a football team on the estate.

Mrs Lucas was the Head Teacher at Kingsmead School, and her husband used to be very keen, so I set up three teams on the estate under eleven, under thirteen and under fifteen football teams. The Head Mistress's husband used to run the under eleven and I was running the under thirteens and fifteens.

We had a full football team going, serious practise matches, and things like that and they were pretty good. We had very good teams in all age groups, in actual fact, I think in the first year we could have win the local league which we came second, I think it was the under fifteens. The under thirteen didn't do badly either and so was the under eleven and probably was in the top five, or somewhere there. But we were all rather pleased about it actually to do something for the youngsters.

I was very strict. I said "If anybody misbehave they will not be playing, no matter how good you are, you will not be playing in any of the team. If we know that you are disrespectful to people, especially the older people". And they realise that I was very strict about that. I'm not saying that all the football vandalism was stopped in a sense but most of it had stopped.

We had the whole of the Hackney Marsh, and sometimes we go over the Mabley Green and we practice over there. There is enough room to practise. We have some of our matches on the Marshes.

It's stopped, quite a long time ago. All of those youngsters they became big young men some have left the estate and gone other places. But it did a lot of good not that it did cut out all the vandalism, I'll say, because not everybody was interested in football. But most of those young men who used to play, they have friends and you know they talk. Some of them would come and watch the match anyway and their parents would come and watch as well, which was good.

Campaigning

It was known that Kingsmead was one of the strongest TA's in Hackney, and over the years I was always invited to go to other TA's who was probably getting a bit folded up or wasn't strong. You got to go and talk with them and say it's important that we have a strong TA. But the onus was actually on the GLC then, to do something, to improve our estate. But apart from finding facilities for the elderly people and things for the youngsters to do, we were a campaigning TA for better facilities on the estate.

In those days we have the rubbish shutes, which were very small and as times goes by a lot of rubbish became a lot and the shute wasn't big enough to take the rubbish down. Therefore people were blocking up the shutes, and people were also dropping things on the stairs, which was a bit of an eyesore.

We contacted the GLC and said "Look we need to have something done, the shutes need to be bigger", and they wouldn't do anything. So we decided to take the GLC to court.

I can't remember the date now but we took the GLC to court, Highbury Corner Magistrate Court. We make our case there about the condition on the estate and that the TA is furious that, you know in this day and age that we, people leaving rubbish on the stairs and the reason for it was because the local GLC didn't provide the facilities. We believe we won the case.

I think it was the Stipendiary Judge at the time saying how the decision is that nobody wins. You can't say you win or you'll win. All I would ask is that you two would go back again, sit down and discuss it because you both have a good argument.

So we went back and the GLC decided we'd do something and put up two new shutes, which was a bit bigger than the normal one. But apart from that we used to have problem with refuse collecting and we keep reporting that the dustcart hasn't come round to collect anything and if you don't we going to take direct action on this.

So we informed the GLC they wasn't doing what we think they should so we decided, the TA that is, decided "Yes" we're going to take direct action. Now direct action was fill up the black bags that we have, take the rubbish, and dump it at the GLC office in Homer Road, E9.

We informed the local newspaper, the Hackney Gazette, we were going to do this thing and we all meet and we load up our plastics bags with rubbish, march in Homerton Road down to Kenworthy Road and then down to Homer Road and all that rubbish we dump it on the steps.

I said, "if you don't do anything, we're going to come back again and do the same". So it was impressive, all in the press, local press at the time. The Hackney Gazette used to report it so we had good prominence in there and actually local councillors and everybody know of Kingsmead.

So we, yea we did things like that on our own. Like we said it never improved a lot but at least when we talk to them we have the privilege then to meet with those officers, who probably never feel like meeting us but they are forced to meet with us.

Because of the activities on Kingsmead that we do there was the London Tenants Organisation, and then the GLC was looking for two people to sit on their Housing Committee at County Hall to represent the tenants in London. At that time we had a hundred thousand tenants on GLC property in London. So they write to the TA and ask if they could nominate somebody. Right away I know they was going to nominate me. So they nominate me to sit on the GLC Housing Committee and one person from Southeast London, was a lady. I can't remember her name and so both of us were the two people who sits on the GLC Housing Committee as the voice of the tenants in London for GLC tenants.

I did that and it helped the voice of Kingsmead and other TA's in Hackney and also in London as a whole. We made our views known as to what is happening to Kingsmead tenants as GLC tenants, and is happening to other GLC tenants round about in London as well. It was good.

Sherries Wharf was built on the side of Kingsmead and they wanted to separate it from Kingsmead and I said, "Well you know, you call it Sherries Wharf but it still Kingsmead". Although some tenants from Kingsmead would say Sherries Wharf is different from Kingsmead. But some of the tenants from Kingsmead did move to Sherries Wharf, but we had to have a big fight on that. Because at the time the GLC was run by the Tories who did not listen to tenants views.

Sherries Wharf is right on the side of the River Lea, it's a good site, you know living beside the river, it's wonderful. They were trying to get people from outside to come and live there. When we realise that we said "No way". So we the TA put our foot down. You know there's tenants in Hackney who can live there or tenants from this estate can go over there. So we had a big struggle with them. So that make them realise, I'm not saying other people shouldn't come but we ensure that most of the people on Kingsmead got a look in.

At one time you know we the TA objected to it becoming all black and other ethnic mixed, not as when I came first. When the GLC hand it over to the council (Hackney) we find that the Local Authority was sending a whole a lot of ethnic people onto the estate and we said, "Stop, no way". You know it used to be a mixed estate with a good mixing of black and white people down here. We do not want it to be flooded with ethnic people down here. So we really had a go at the council and we stopped it. We remember Edwy House it was black and white and next thing I know there it was only blacks on there. We said, "No, no we want it to be mixed", because if you look at the committee here it was very mixed.

There was bad things happened on the Kingsmead. One morning I got up to go to work and on the door there was a big NF written on it. It was reported in the West Indian World newspaper at the time who came down and they photographed it. We called the Police, it take a long time for the Police to come but they came.

Community work

Before the estate was modernised as it is now, if you in those 1970s or 1980s go into someone's flats to see how the tenants they really keep there place wonderful, really nice. I will tell you this that many have wonderful, clean lovely places. There, it is their palace, it is our palace I would say.

I used to know almost every flat on the estate. Because I used to be the one who would drop a newsletter off to the tenants I would run up the stairs and many people used to invite me into their homes in the old days. They would say come in. It wasn't anything looking like what it looks like now.

People always say there was bad things going on here. In those days youngsters used to be very mischievous and break windows but nothing as what is happening today. I cannot remember anybody has ever coming to say, you know, there is a group of boys whom they saw smoking drugs, or there is a group of boys breaking in a house to steal money so they can get drugs. Apart from the few, most youngsters because the appearance of them on the estate and the appearance of the next door neighbour is there, so most of them have some sort of respect for those people.

My relationship on Kingsmead with the people of Kingsmead was pretty good and I have no regrets at all. I became a councillor in 1982. It was in this ward, Kings Park Ward. So when the nomination came, I won the nomination and when the election came I won the election. I polled the highest number of votes ever in Kings Park Ward.

The community's future

When the King and Queen opening this estate, in those days Kingsmead estate was the top. Now it is not run by local authority now it is a housing association that run this now. People who I have spoke to are very pleased about it and I'm only hoping that people see it as such a transformation on the estate and they treat like that. At the moment I could see a lot of people doing something to make certain it stayed like that. They have a good flower pots and things in the area.

I see some people throw things about which making it look untidy and I thought please, don't let it be like in the past when people dumped things, you know. Keep it as its wonderful now, its so wonderful now. I just hope that people will treat it that way. Your home is your home, treat you home as your own palace.

When people live off the estate and I say, "Have you been down to Kingsmead?" They say "I haven't been but I have heard about it and how it has changed so much', and I say, "It's nice".

Sid and Eve Mecoy

Both Sid and Eve have a long history of being actively involved in community organisations and groups since they came onto the estate from the nearby Nye Bevan Estate in 1989. Sid was Secretary of the Tenants Association, and Eve was treasurer. Both are currently involved in running the Over 50's Club.
They have a caravan on Canvey Island with other 'Eastenders' where they spend most of their summers and where they eventually hope to move to.

From Nye Bevan Estate TA to Kingsmead Estate TA
I had an argument with the Council, I was Secretary of Nye Bevan TA at the time and I was fighting for people's rights down there.

We had all the scaffolding up and they shut all the gardens off at the back, we couldn't use no gardens or anything.

They wanted to get me out, and they got me out on account that I wasn't at work at the time. I haven't been able to work for ages now and they were still mucking about with their rent policy, rent rebates and all that business. They said I was in arrears but then in the end they cleared it all up, but it was too late then.

I was Secretary of Nye Bevan TA for seventeen years, but twenty seven years as a member of the TA. When I took over at Kingsmead it was a bit of a state. People just sort of pushed me to it, I think it's because I gas too much. I'm not frightened to speak my mind. I think that's like that and I don't agree in shouting and hollering, never have done because I find the moment you start hollering and shouting, that's all you're doing, you're giving everything over to the person who you're shouting at, they know that they have won. If you keep steady and that, you find that you beat them the opposite way by you being steady and they're the ones that end up ranting and raving.

Apart from being Secretary of the TA and my missus, Eve, she was Treasurer at the time, we've been doing the Over 50's Club which we're both involved in as Secretary and Treasurer again, but in reverse roles this time.

The other things that we was involved in was when we used to have the Hackney Marsh Festival when it first started, I was on the committee of that. It's got to be late 70's, early 80's or something like that, we started The Marsh Fun Festival. I mean that's how we got the playground over here because it was funded from out of the money that we made from the Hackney Marsh Fun Festival.

The very first one, we had fifty four floats which was all round Kingsmead Way and right through to Mare Street then back to Kingsmead Way where they would make out the decision who had the best float and everything like that.

I don't know how it actually started. We had one quick meeting down at Nye Bevan Hall and then after that it was held in a person's basement in Rushmore Road, there was a load of us just got together and suggested it. Derek Fleming was one, Alan, it was in his house, in his cellar and then we got Free Form (arts project) involved so that was there and they was the ones that helped getting it all really going on and everything like that because we had no idea.

When the GLC got finished we had problems with funding because the GLC used to fund us for our marquees and all these tables.

We had Lesneys, they used to give us money, we had the Hackney Gazette free advertising plus some money, then we had

Metal Box Company used to give us money. The other one was the wood place, Lathams, they used to supply round about seven or eight lorries for floats, plus other things as well. The drivers used to give up their time for free.

Then people didn't want to know, it just cost money, we can't do that and of course as you know we lost Metal Box up there, we lost Lesneys in the sense of the word so it just wasn't there.

Then the council wanted to charge us so much to use the field over here that's why in the end it ended up by Hackney Hospital. We had them up there, for about three or four years we done that and then like a lot of us we get a lot older and we can't do all this stuff.

The younger ones, they like going to these places but they don't like getting involved putting it up, especially when you didn't get paid for it. I mean staying in tents overnight to make sure nothing gets vandalised or anything like that, you know what I mean?

We also got outings and stuff where we took the children and the parents out, it was only down to Southend but we had coaches taking them down to Southend for the day. On those occasions we got the money from the council.

In the 70's, and early 80's, in the 90's there was a bit of an uprising by some of the tenants on the estate in which they all got together and made the Police and the council work together and we got some of these unruly elements sorted out. Where we used to have six to eight burglaries a day, now from what I can make out there's probably about six or eight burglaries perhaps every three months or something like that now, at least reported ones. But there was a big difference from when it was six and eight a day.

Challenging negative images

I think people are seeing the estate, from what I've seen or I've heard from other people it's, "Cor I went past your estate, don't it look different now? It looks better". Now I'm getting that feeling from there and as I say, when it's all done it will look nice but you know what I mean, it's there like that. But I still think Kingsmead somehow or the other has still got to lose that image of what it was and everything like that.

I've tried it a couple of times when I've been involved with the radio and the television. I've said, that it's about time the people were starting to give people on Kingsmead a bit of credit, they're not all thieves and goodness knows what. Let them have catalogues, all right there's plenty of people not in the higher bracket of money side of it, where they use all these catalogues and goodness knows what, but the catalogues are being now used on this estate. If you lived on Kingsmead it was a black market and you couldn't get anything unless you was already involved when you come on like, you know what I mean?

Challenges for the community

I hope the estate goes upwards, really upwards. It will probably go up if people know how to control their own houses and keep them tidy and everything like that. I feel sorry for people on the ground floor, I mean they sling stuff out of the window and it's going into their gardens. Or when they start washing carpets out, they sling it over the top of the balcony, anybody up the top, if anybody leans over like that and they're getting all the wet from the carpet down on them and all the kiddies, they shake their carpet over the top. Now that's a thing that people have got to stop doing because I think it just degrades the estate one way or the other.

It's got to be a better estate especially if they get all the cameras (CCTV) working properly and everything like that.

We know quite a few of our neighbours. We keep to ourselves quite a bit though now after all these years but we can't walk through the estate without people calling out to you though. The people next door to here are new, fair enough they haven't been long there, we haven't seen them much but they seem all right. Up there, a couple of doors up there they're all right.

At the moment I think the estate is all right as long as we can get the parents to know how to look after their children. Now I'm not against children, I've worked with children for thirty years or so, but there's some parents that don't know how to look after their children. They just let them roam and do what they like, that thing is still carrying on and also it's how do you teach tenants to look after the properties that's all been done up for them. That's my honest opinion.

It's gradually coming round to a bit more community but I think once all the refurbishment is done, I think this is where we can all get together somehow or other and start working together. I like to see more activities for people, especially the youth on the estate.

Moving to Canvey Island

If everything works out right we can move down to Canvey Island we'd be down there like a shot, that would have happened many years ago as well if it had happened but we're still waiting. If we get the chance of anything down at Canvey, we've got our caravan there, and we love it down there, we've got friends down there left, right and centre so we wouldn't be on our own like.

Canvey is made up of Eastenders. The people that we've met down there and I'm talking about a hell of a lot of people we've met, you find that they've come from Tottenham, Stoke Newington,

Stanford Hill, Clapton, Hackney, Bethnal Green, all round Stepney, Barking, Dagenham, they're all there, they've all moved down there. I mean there's so many. Some have been down there thirty to forty years, Canvey is the Eastender's paradise. You know we're always saying let's win the lottery one day so we can buy a house down there.

Ron Newman

During the years Ron lived on the estate he was a member of the Tenants Association and Chair of the Kingsmead Trust. He was a leading figure in the community during the transfer process leading to Kingsmead Homes Housing Association taking over the estate from the local authority.
Ron is currently Chair of Disability Hackney and is involved in disability forums and issues across London. He has recently

received a human rights award for his work with people with disabilities.

Getting involved

Hackney at the time was a really poor landlord, the housing stock was awful so I got myself asking from the community minded point of view how can I get involved, is there a TA, what does the TA do. So I got involved with fun days and things like that. That's before I went into a wheelchair and unfortunately five years later I had a stroke by doing too much work but I don't look at my disability as I must give up.

Working with tenants

They've always had a Tenants Association, I got involved when I lived on the estate but when the regeneration development was coming along I got involved with the Board of Kingsmead Homes Limited and then obviously I attended public meetings and things like that.

Jack Straw came because we had a NACRO Report done and basically it was about crime, life on the estate, resident's views, and the media and the stigma it brought. It was just some sort of report the Council wanted done because it was basically a tick against their names and saying look at what they're doing for the residents.

I did a speech. I wasn't kind to the Council. I basically said they really let the residents down and that then boom, the media then came back attacking me, asking me questions at my door at 7.30 in the morning, on the radio, on the TV.

I didn't mind because I thought it's about time that Hackney Council were told you may have done this report but we didn't want this report, you wanted the report. I want to know from my point of view as a resident what are you going to do to bring our homes and bring our estate to be a more community inviting estate. Then it came out, the plan was to sell it off to the housing association.

You had a man called Abdul, he was basically like Mr Everybody, he was one of these really nice residents who minded his own business and cared for the community, he was the Tenants Association Chairman. We became firm friends because we both had a passion for our community.

He lived at one end and I lived at the other, so he looked after that side and I looked after my side. It was brilliant and since then he's moved on and had a family and I don't know where he's gone, but now and again I still get a phone call from him or a letter from him.

It's pleasing to see like he still keeps in contact and he was such a great guy, he was one of the characters. Kingsmead loved having him around, any problems they'd knock on his door because like he wanted to get rid of the stigma of the 'estate from hell' that Kingsmead has always been like in the media.

Setting up the youth club

Back in '93 my wife Miriam said to people 'Let's set up a youth club if we can get a derelict hall'. The hall was already there, where the café is, the Kingsmead Hall behind, but the Council needed to pump money into it to get it up to health and safety scratch. It was only used by one lady on a Sunday who was adamant she wasn't letting anyone use the hall.

The Council duly put up a fight, first of all they said 'No' and we kept saying "Why not? Our children deserve a hall". We used the media as much as we could to fight for that so in the end they agreed and we got all the young kids together on a Saturday and said "Right kids, what do you want to do with the hall?"

A few of us went round to speak to the older ones, they come up with ridiculous things like weight-training and bicycle tracks, you know things that the older ones would want, but they did agree to have the table-tennis and pool and things like that, and that's where we started working together.

We opened a youth club. Setting up the youth services for the kids because they really needed it, rather than getting into trouble with the neighbours or the Police, trying to make their life better.

So we set up the youth club, got youth workers, got crime prevention workers, had various people, a load of MP's, we had Jack Straw down here, and we had a Minister from Sweden down here.

The estate transfer

The Council we're going to sell on the eighteen estates and Kingsmead was the very first one. Being Kingsmead, they thought it would be the baby of everything, this is the way the future should be like for the residents.

At the time when the process bidding was on and it was who we were supposed to go for, Peabody Trust or Kingsmead Homes, or stay with the Council, Kingsmead Homes came out strongest. At the time I was part of the working party with the Council.

If some question came to both Peabody and Kingsmead Homes, Kingsmead Homes came out the stronger but deep down in my own heart I wish I'd never went out and said to the residents vote Kingsmead, this is a good deal. Because Peabody are obviously the more stronger housing association around the borough and they're doing vastly more community minded things than Kingsmead Homes.

There's no use having a housing association having an office and doing nothing for your community, you need a housing association that's going to be community-minded by setting up projects with the likes of the Kabin or the TA or Wally Foster. Like Peabody Housing Association do, they've got their own sort of funding elements and bringing the community into it, sadly I don't think Kingsmead Homes have done that.

I wish there was another way of bringing more better regeneration to Kingsmead than the current state of play. If Kingsmead Homes were more open-minded like they said they would be in their bid, if they followed their original bid, even to look at it today, they've not achieved what they said.

They may say in their mind we achieved it but from a resident's point of view and an outsider, I'm hearing every day what's going on, it's like they haven't said what they set up to do which is wrong.

I was more in favour when there was the regeneration to bulldoze the estate and rebuild it that would have been my choice. When they told us it couldn't be done because of a, b and c, then we had to have a refurbishment inside and outside the estate, which is massive and ongoing.

Already five years have gone by and it's still not completed because of various problems in-between.

Civil action against tenants

Kingsmead Estate has had a really rough ride in the media. When sort of like the anti-social behaviour of residents was here, the press were down just like that and what made matters worse at the time was that they done a drama on BBC Panorama.

A couple of my neighbours was beaten up in their homes. It was families like doing it, and then with residents working with the Council and the Police together, how can we combat this crime in making people want to live on the Mead rather than people wishing to move off the Mead.

Because back in 1993 everybody wanted to move off, but not me. I said, "It's about time us residents stood up to them", and we did.

The problem was that those residents didn't want to go up into the court. So we could understand their point of view, the next-door-neighbours saying I can't finger him or her. But then something happened between the Council and the Police and they got removed. But you can see those children today, you wouldn't think they were the same kids, they've got families, they've got grandchildren, its just like hello are you still the same person.

Obviously a couple of them done time inside, when they came out they actually thanked me and Miriam for basically doing time and they said "We'll never do it again" and they don't, we see them now shopping and even running their own shops.

Reflections: Living off the estate

I was sad, I was very sad to read about the break-in of the Concorde (youth club), I sent an e-mail and I said 'I hope you get the thugs, whoever they were'. Me and my wife couldn't believe it.

There's gangs there but there's always been gangs around Kingsmead, you'll never get rid of it but maybe the youth workers can deal with that side of it. You know no-one knows, I wish I knew why they hang out and what's the perception of hanging around in a gang, what buzz do you get out of doing this, doing this crime, is it good fun, are you bored? But again you see all these questions are going to be asked by the youth workers.

I hope it gets better, I really do. I hope they can one day get a really recognised strong TA to be the voice of the people, to get rid of the stigma. People that's on the TA that I hear about, that isn't a proper TA, getting those people who don't agree with what Kingsmead Homes are doing. So I really would like to see more people at the end of the day say to Kingsmead Homes we're not happy with this because. We used to have a weekly walk around, looking at maintenance and stairs and general things but I don't know if that happens anymore.

People want to live on it, I mean I've got people round my community, when they said to me "What was Kingsmead like when you lived on there?" I said "It was a very happy time for us", and it's "Well I've got friends in there and I'd like to live there".

But other people that I've seen on Kingsmead, they want to get off for one reason or another and that's down to them but you know I get a tear every time I drive past the estate, I really do but that's me and my family. The way it was done was sad but that's the way it goes sometimes.

I lived on the estate for eleven years, since 1985 until the 90's, sadly due to my disability I had to move off. I enjoyed my eleven years on here, I wish I could move back. Me and my wife felt there was a sense of community, and we built up relationships with other tenants.

I do really miss the old residents when I see them. We only hope that when they do finish it and they have some type of an event and they try and put a press release in the local paper and say 'Anybody who lived on the estate between these years' or 'If you were a Board member', 'Get in touch, we'd like to invite you as guests'. I hope, but I can't see that happening to be honest. I had a lot of time for the community but now I don't.

Everything that I fought for as a resident of Hackney with the transfer, we were going to have a lovely home, have a garden, have a car space, everything that we wanted basically and we never saw it. You know it's sad, we drove into the concourse last night, me and the wife and she was crying because she wishes she could come back. That was what we wanted.

Brian Powell

An Cambridge undergraduate Brian moved onto the estate in 1977. He has always taken a keen interest in the history of the estate and has been active in his local church and on the estate for most of the years he has lived there. Brian is currently a School Governor at a local school.

Tenants Association

The establishment of the Tenants Association went back to the 1970s and the activities of St Paul's Homerton Church, which is now Christchurch who now worship at the Wally Foster centre. The church was very influential and Jack Shepherd who was working for the GLC as a Housing Officer, lived on the Mead and he, as a churchman, was involved with the early days of Christchurch on the Mead.

He also contacted people like former councillor Ken Hanson who now has bought a house round the corner but who then lived on the Mead and there was some very good West Indians, a man called Paul Griffiths, who were mostly men of religious faith as well and they had got together to organise a Tenants Association.

By the time I arrived here the Wally Foster community centre was just up and running. This had been in response to demands from the Tenants Association because there was only the Golden Shoe pub. That was the only kind of social centre so the Wally Foster Centre had been built.

Part of the demands of the tenant's organisation, led to building the Wally Foster centre. There were a lot of the mums, West Indians, and some of the old and established white English mums who were around who were very much into children's parties who were involved with the Tenants Association at the time, going back to the 1970s.

They organised a number of events for the kids in Silver Jubilee year, but also they always organised things like a Christmas party for the kids round at the Wally Foster Centre, this went on until the 80s.

Then the TA became very politicised. The TA focussed on dealing with specific political problems such as housing, such as the affect of cutbacks on education, such as the affect of cutbacks in what now is called Income Support but was then known I think as Supplementary Benefit. This rather froze out of the TA the women who wanted it just to be there to raise funds and do things with the kids.

In the late 80s, when I was Chairman of the Tenants Association, we had a major issue with Bengalis/Bangladeshis. They were being given flats on the estate and had no command, or very little command of English and needed a lot of support which was not always forthcoming in those days. Although the Council did begin to try to provide interpreters, but too little too late in a way.

It was an issue for the Tenants Association to be aware that these incoming Bangladeshi families had many needs and they couldn't speak the language so it was quite difficult. Then a godsend arrived in the form of a young Bangladeshi man who had been born and brought up in Glasgow who we communicated with. This guy he really spoke Scots with a Glasgow thick accent. But that didn't matter because we could tell him what we wanted to ask these families and to try to find out what we needed to advise them on which he would do.

As Chair of the Tenants Association it proved almost impossible to, except in a very small way compared to how it had been, to crank up the interest and commitment of people.

One time however when I was Chair we had a meeting about the issue of asbestos that had been used in a number of the flats in wall coverings and in cement. One of the places where there had been asbestos was when they did the package improvements. Because people no longer needed their open fires and there were complaints about the open fires being a source of pollution, the soot would come down into the rooms and the chimneys weren't being swept.

It was not uncommon to have a soot fall or smoke penetration into the house and with the package improvements they had taken out the old fireplaces and sealed the holes with asbestos containing plasterboard.

As a result of the agitation we had a firm of asbestos removers come in and these fibreboard panels were removed.

Although it has got much better, there have been from time to time people who would create inappropriate levels of noise. As Chair I got a call from a woman, she lived over in Templemead House, and there was a young guy living on one of the top floors up there and he was for a time trying to run an illegal nightclub from his place.

He installed this sound equipment, which pumped out very loud noisy music, and we had a stream of people, couples and single men and women making their way to the flat and partying up there until all hours. She was actually at the end of her tether from the noise that this was making. I was sitting on the edge of her sofa and the vibration from the three floors above was actually vibrating against the inside of my legs.

Generally it has improved. When you do get noisy parties they are never things that are continually repeated. I think there may be an issue with individual flats though.

In the late 80s under the aegis of the TA and in contact with our local home beat officers, we organised a law and order meeting at the Wally Foster Centre.

We were trying to set up a neighbourhood watch scheme and there was quite a lot of anger from people living around Alfred House and Edgar House. One of the flats, I think in one of those blocks was where the final paedophile party at which Jason Swift was murdered took place.

One of the people who had been living near got quite angry with this Police Inspector who was talking in favour of a neighbourhood watch scheme. He asked how can we be sure it will do us any good because when that party was going on (Jason Swift) we phoned you up and it was three hours later and they had all gone before any Police came near the place and we told you that it was nonce's with kids. So there was criticism of the Police.

Generally when the chips are down the community here will work together. There are people in the community, even if there are people that are difficult to draw in, there has always been a kind of sub-stratum of people who will collaborate together. You can see the network around the Mecoys (Sid and Eve), he ran the

Tenants Association and tenant centre many times and they tend to come into being.

I think in a way there always has been a sense of community, but I think it is patchy. I think there are still probably quite a lot of people who feel isolated or are less able to access the community that exists. I think there are many people who probably would give you an answer that there isn't and yet they are in their own networks. Anybody who wants to nurture the sense of community on the estate has to understand how it is a network of networks and how there may be networks that have community within their own yet don't feel they have links with other people, they are in fact part of the community but don't feel it.

Estate landlords

This place was built for the working class. You can see the old attitude, which meant that when Kingsmead was built nobody had the wit to think that the working class might want refrigerators, which were beginning to come in. Nobody thought they needed any more space in their kitchens than for an old fashioned butler sink, and somewhere they could put a gas boiler, and somewhere they could put a gas cooker.

Originally the landlord was the London County Council (LCC) and then in the 1960s it was the Greater London Council who took over from the LCC. The estates were transferred over to Hackney in the early 1980s, some years before the actual demise of the GLC.

The GLC, whatever its faults, was a much more effective landlord. Those who wanted to make trouble for them and criticise them could point to and say they were wasting money and their costs of administration were much higher per property, because of their size they at least had access to a range of staff. However they could call on a range of skills, which unfortunately over the years got diluted as people retired, or financial cutbacks meant they had to re-jig their system

The GLC was a good positive experience. They were very efficiently managed. If you missed a rent payment for a couple of weeks and very often after a week, there was a letter from your Housing Manager pointing it out and there was an invitation to come and talk to him.

When we went over to Hackney (Council) that kind of fell by the wayside because again they were trying to manage it at a time of cutbacks and they had reduced staff and Hackney has never been particularly efficient in collecting rents and things like that. There was a marked deterioration in many aspects.

Then Kingsmead Homes became our landlord. I hear anecdotes from people who are not 100% happy with Kingsmead Homes. For example, a friend of mine who is in the final phase over the other side, she has a tremendous lot of stuff in her flat and with myself should have had a de-camp to another flat. She has had to fight them tooth and nail to get even a partial de-camp where they have put some of her stuff in store and she is still supposed to be in there with a considerable amount of stuff left and with all the dust and everything like that.

So that is one thing that I have direct experience of and one has those anecdotes of people suggesting that Kingsmead Homes doesn't always deliver in terms of people's expectations, especially in view of the fact that it is advertised as a Christian company. Maybe people are putting unrealistic expectations on them.

My experience has been ok. I am a slightly biased because for many years I have been involved on the Management Board of Kingsmead Homes.

They do have a closer working relationship with the Police. On a number of occasions, certainly when I was on the Board a couple of years ago, it reported to us where if anybody is a really bad tenant, if they are say drug dealing or using their flat as a base for crime, or maybe even prostitution, Kingsmead Homes would get a professional witness company to actually get a case against them and they will find themselves down in Shoreditch County Court.

With Kingsmead Homes, the whole estate is much more tightly managed, there is much better control of voids. This was a real problem. Back in the 1970s if somebody moved out of a flat and the Council didn't come round that day and put up the security grills the local kids would break in there that evening. Not necessarily to steal anything because there might not be anything to steal, but simply breaking in to keep their hand in.

It was very notable that until about three or four years ago any time there was a reference to the estate in the press it was 'the notorious Kingsmead estate'. More recently, in the last year, things have been better. It is now 'the once notorious' or 'formerly notorious Kingsmead estate' and one or two people that I have met that live in other parts of Hackney have said 'I was down Kingsmead, it hasn't half changed, its much better'. So I think slowly there is a change in perception.

As the refurbishment gets completed and then there will be the landscaping and visually it looks better. I see myself living here as long as I am absolutely capable of, barring accidents like suddenly accessing some great wealth or something like that whereby I might well wish to move, but I see myself continuing to live here.

6. Living and Working on the Estate

Not many people live and work in the same small geographical community particularly if the media has seen it as one of the worst inner-city housing estates in England. Bob Holman's name comes to mind as one of the few exceptions, with his mixture of community work, written reflections and decision to live with his family in his workplace firstly on the Southdown Housing Estate in Bath, and then Easterhouse, Glasgow (Holman, 1981, 1998).

This makes Ann Davies's story the more interesting. As an outsider and new to London's East End she became both a volunteer with the Kabin Project on the estate and moved into one of the flats. Her experiences of coming from a different background to most of the tenants, the process of slowly becoming accepted and welcomed by people, working with young people and families, and experiencing as a member of the community a critical period of the estates history with its change of landlord are captured in her story.

Ann Davies

Ann came to the estate in 1995 as a full-time volunteer family worker with the Kabin Project. Previously she lived in Birmingham for four years and had got involved in local community activities as a student.
As an outsider it initially took her some time to be accepted by the community as someone who both lived and worked on the estate.
Ann now works locally for the London Borough of Hackney as a qualified social worker with children and young people but is still involved in estate issues.

Coming on to the estate
The vicar at the local church on the estate, which meets at the Wally Foster Centre, was looking for a volunteer for the Kabin, which has now become the Hackney Marsh Partnership. So I basically came here to be a full-time volunteer. I got board and lodging, and a flat on the estate because they had an agreement with Hackney Council. The church had volunteers, they had to volunteer for a year. We all moved to this flat, so I came and shared with two other people.

The first two years on the estate were almost life changing. I think it was really linked to me working on the estate as well and living on the estate. It was quite a new environment for me.

I'd lived in the inner city in Birmingham for four years and I had got involved in local community activities as a student. Then I went to a really small church and did a youth club there and went off at weekends with the church and the kids there. But it wasn't until I came here that I really was living in a community like this 24/7.

The Kabin was just starting at the time, we just had one of the shop fronts and when I came it was still being finished off. The Post Office came and renovated it free.

We were just opening up and we were developing all these ideas for projects and thinking about how we could use the space and what people in the community would want to have there. It was just all new and exciting, and I was really part of that and so I got to know loads of people just by being down there.

Being accepted by the community

I don't think I ever felt that people weren't accepting me. But I did feel that, I suppose when I first came to Kingsmead, I felt very conscious of my accent. I thought that maybe I didn't know how they would perceive me, but maybe that was my worry.

There were all sorts of people living on the estate and I think I felt a bit middle class and conscious of that, and also coming in as a sort of as a worker Into the Kabin, I was quite conscious I had to earn peoples respect. I think that's true of anything in any area, you can't just come to a place and expect people to like you who have been here for years.

I was just trying to be myself and I think people were really friendly. I think I got to know people mainly through the Kabin at first and since then I suppose, I've got to know my neighbours and I feel like I know people in my own right now. At first it was very much, "Ann works at the Kabin", and people knew me in that role.

There was a bit of an overlap because people knew, especially people in these two blocks that I lived here and they see me as a neighbour as well, and that's started to develop friendships and people then see me as a friend.

So it just took time and I do feel that pretty much that people are friendly, you get to know some nice people and to know my neighbours. You chat to people. I think people have been friendly to me.

There used to be a grocery shop that's now a Turkish shop, used to be called Ronnie's. Ronnie and his son Robert and an elderly lady called Kathy, who was Scottish who worked there, they just knew everyone. They had been there for years and years. It was a real sort of community, a focal point in a way.

You didn't go inside the shop, you didn't necessarily know that until you got to know the rules. When I first went I walked in and you didn't do that, everyone queued outside on the pavement and then they had all the fruit and veg and stuff on the front and everything else inside, you sort of asked for it and they brought it out. Everyone used to laugh and joke with everyone.

Youth work

I started doing youth work, I was sort of seconded, when I was a full time volunteer at the Kabin. There was a junior club at the Kingsmead Trust a couple of afternoons after school with eight to thirteens. It was quite a normal sort of youth club thing, you know snooker, football, pool, table tennis activities, painting. I remember everyone was making Batman out of balsa wood. We did cooking and we had a couple of youth workers there. We had a visit from the Duke of Edinburgh once, he was coming round, because he was part of the London Federation of Youth Clubs and it was affiliated to that. That was really an unusual day loads and loads of people came to the club that wouldn't normally come. It was really staged, like we had all these activities that we never normally would have.

All the parents came plus I was doing cookery in the kitchen. The Duke of Edinburgh tried a banana milkshake and one of the mums had a real go at him about poverty and had a real shout at him here, which was interesting.

The junior work moved onto the Concorde and I carried on with that for a while for about a year. I think that was really excellent and at first when I went round I was a bit scared. I was like this white woman, you know slightly posh voice and then it was a predominantly black youth club and all the kids were streetwise and all the language that they used.

I just hung in there and gradually I'm just trying to be myself especially as much as possible and just got to know the people and I did get to know them and I think it was alright. I think I did get accepted after a while.

About three years I was sort of doing bits and pieces of youth work not loads but now I really feel that I can just see kids walking around the estate that I can say hello to, have a little chat with and they'll still be like "Alright then? You OK? How are you?" Like the other day I got a new washing machine and I couldn't get it out of the lift and about three of them came and helped me. I'm really glad that I can at least say "hello". It kind of means something.

Supporting neighbours

I do like the fact that I know people. You just say "Hi" to your neighbours and you walk into the courtyard and there is always going to be people you know. The flip side of that is that you sometimes feel you don't have any privacy because as soon as you walk out everyone sees you.

Just living here has opened my eyes to so many things. I've met so many different people from different cultures and all different walks of life, and different experiences. Some of who have had to put up with a lot and who live in really difficult circumstances.

A family, who used to live on the estate, in the block opposite, this Bengali family with six kids, I got to know them really quite well. I consider them to be good friends now. They've actually moved from the estate because they had really bad racial harassment.

I got to know them initially through the Kabin but then I developed a friendship with them that was outside of that, in my spare time. I got to know the kids and the mum. The kids always used to be in the courtyard and always when I used to come home from Tesco's in the car they all just used to come out the house and then run to help me carry the shopping. They used to come out at the weekend and tell me what they did at school.

I didn't know they were having so many problems to start with. But then the mum started having all these threats. Like people knocking on the front door in the middle of the night, breaking the glass and just being really abusive. Saying they were going to kill her and had a knife and stuff. So she started ringing me whenever it happened so she would ring me at half one or two in the morning to say "Can you come down I've just had someone banging on my door".

I would just like go down in my pyjamas to the block opposite and sit with her. I don't know you know that kind of thing opens your eyes to what people have to experience. Your know the good and the bad. They are such a lovely family and they are really good friends of mine now I've known the kids. But I have also seen what they had to deal with and that's really tough.

Kingsmead Homes

When I first came we were still voting for the transfer, whether to transfer from the council. That felt like there was a sort of series of events happening. You know big meetings on how housing associations work, and giving presentations and we would all go to hear them. Things have changed absolutely loads since all that happened. Because all the works have started. For the last however many years it is, five years, you just get used to living in this building site and constant change. Doing the road or doing the blocks opposite you or doing your own block, or the other block or the courtyard.

The actual process of dealing with the work was horrible, and it still is. There still are people in a complete state of turmoil over it and desperately upset and really angry and frustrated about the way that they have been treated. The process and the way they've gone about it has been quite damaging and has really exploited tenants.

They (Kingsmead Homes) talked about consulting the tenants and listening and doing all those things but basically for a money saver, they chose to do the building works with tenants still in their flats. It was completed in different phases. We were in phase two and there was a lot of problems with phase one and a lot of the tenants got together and tried to take action and got the health and safety people down.

At one point they got the work stopped, the Kabin was involved in that. They were just appalled by the workmen coming in and they were living in the flats. There were families living there, workmen coming in and taking your toilet and bedroom doors and expecting people to live like that for twelve weeks.

Everyone's got a story, its like if you meet someone and they say "I'm having my flat done" and then they start and say what's happened to them you know, everyone else just goes "Oh yeah, that happened to me".

What happened to us, was they damaged loads of our stuff. You felt like you had no voice. You felt like you were nothing. You complained to the contractors and they come up with all this stuff, all these promises you know it was covered by our insurance. I wrote letters and then we wrote to Kingsmead Homes and got all the usual stuff you know. The workmen just had free reign of the flat and I have just heard so many stories of people having things stolen or broken.

I cannot imagine how people coped. They do the work when you're living in it, because it's just absolutely chaos, everything the dust, the dirt.

Obviously having Kingsmead Homes on site that has changed because we used to have to go to the Housing Office on the Lower Clapton Road. I think everyone thought that would be really excellent, because when the Council owned it took ages to get repairs done. But it hasn't been the best if I'm honest. It's still quite difficult to get things done.

The physical appearance of the estate has changed dramatically and I think it looks a lot better now. From an aesthetic point of view I think it looks a lot better especially those blocks over there, Egbert House and Alfred House, they used to look really grim.

But I think it does look a lot nicer. When you come home from work and you go to the courtyard area in the middle of the two blocks it just feels so much better and the way the have landscaped it, you do feel you are coming home.

The insides of the flats are nice although there is a bit of shoddy workmanship. Overall I think I'm quite pleased with how it is.

A difficult summer

Recently it's been quite bad on the estate. This summer has been really awful and everyone that lives in this block that I see and that I pass on the stairs are really fed up with it, it's really horrible. There is loads of graffiti all over the stairs and the lifts are broken now. It's been broken every week of the summer. Maybe it's mended or not. It's kids that are jumping around setting off fireworks in it. Setting things on fire. There are all burn marks on the stairwells and the stairwells are filthy.

There's a lot of kids outside and recently they have been around our balcony and on the stairs and smoking. I'm sure there's a lot of drugs going on and I'm sure some of it is hidden, because a lot of it is out there. A lot of kids hanging around in gangs outside does feel quite intimidating.

I had my car broken into a quite a few times, damaged the windscreen, the windows were smashed. One of my cars was stolen on the estate. I got another car and it got broken into immediately, straight away the day after I got it. It was parked up the road. There was a lot of car thief's, a lot of cars being broken into and joy riding at the time. You hear motor bikes going really fast up and down there and cars and a lot of the kids hanging around and doing that kind of thing. It's really loud some of the time, the estate, sometimes it gets really noisy like with neighbours arguing. Sometimes it's just people living their daily lives you hear it, it's not their fault. You know just walking around and stuff, or loud music. Quite often there's really loud music, it's really anti-social and that grinds you down.

It's okay if it's a one off but when its sort of a constant noise and then its filthy outside and you know when you come home you have to like step past the kids sitting on the stairs to get in. It kind of wears you out a bit and it's just not very pleasant to come home to, but that's been recent.

Before that, when I first came here, I don't think it was quite as bad, I didn't feel like I wasn't seeing a lot of crime, I got burgled in about 1996 but I haven't got burgled since which is good. But recently I have heard of a couple again. So I don't know. It did feel like over the summer it was kind of brewing up again, like there was something going on. It hadn't felt like that for years. I have always felt really comfortable and really safe on the estate, but recently I have been a bit uneasy.

Looking to the future

I think I'd like to see the estate shedding that really bad reputation or starting to shed it. I'd like to think that the physical changes could at last make a difference. It's demoralising when I see that it's just been renovated and coming up our stairs already it's full of graffiti and smashed windows. I think that's a bit disheartening because it's got to be about more. You can't just change the buildings and expect everything to change, you've got to have regeneration as well. You've got to be ready to invest you know, the resources to do.

There used to be a playground area and that has all been ripped out and they are doing it just now and its taken them three years for them to do it and there's been nowhere for the kids to play over that side.

I'd like to see the Tenants Association become strong because that's been a problem as well over the years, that every time there's been a TA it's been fraught with politics and personalities and people getting burnt out. Now the TA has reformed recently and got off to a really good start. I wasn't involved in it because I don't have the energy to do it. That's the thing, I think you do get quite ground down by things.

But I would like to think that in the future we could have a really strong group of tenants that could have a say and have a voice and be able to take decisions and all of that. But it does feel like it's a bit of a losing battle because it's hard for us to act together and to be heard and to sort of mobilise.

It would be good to have that on the estate and for things to continue, for the youth club to be funded, and to have a new playground where the kids can play.

Part of me would really like to stay here and carry on living here because I do feel settled. I feel like I know people and I feel like I'm part of a community, and there are times when I really love that and I get a buzz out of it.

But part of me thinks that if I got my own place then I would like a bit more space and perhaps somewhere where it is a bit quieter. If I do move there will always be a part of me that thinks I should be here, now.

I will always have a real affection for the estate, because I think I came here at a time when you know it sort of shapes a lot of what

I have done, being here has changed me. The experiences that I have had have opened my eyes to so many things.

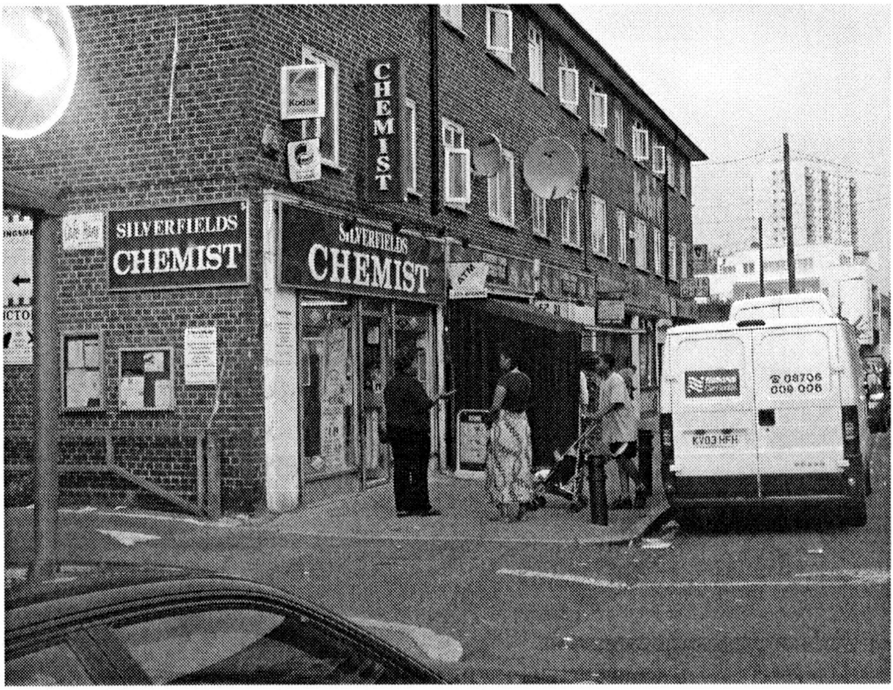

7. Ex-Residents

These three accounts by ex-residents span the period from the Second World War of the 1940's through to the late 1980's. They are a mixture of nostalgia and fleeting impressions, with Connie Reece recalling the estate at the outbreak of war, the importance of the family and being good neighbours, and its working class vibrancy. Brian Cook remembers his childhood, the games played, and how everybody knew everybody, whilst the actor Ewan McGregor was passing through.

Connie Reece MBE

Connie is in her eighties. She lived on the estate in the 1940s. Her family was one of the first families to be rehoused there from slum clearances. She recalls the wartime years on the estate and helping her Jewish neighbours, and the estate's strong working class culture.
Now living in Stevenage, Hertfordshire Connie was awarded the MBE for services for her voluntary and charitable work. She is still actively involved in her community.
Connie recently returned to the estate for a visit.

The Smith family moved to Kingsmead Estate in 1940 to a four bedroom flat on the first floor, we were a family of six children. I was twenty awaiting my twenty first birthday. The flats were only four storey's high with a laundry room and waste disposal chute. We had lived in a very small house in Shoreditch, a two or three bedroom house. The area was getting ready for demolition at the time so we were moved onto the Kingsmead estate.

The Hackney Marshes made the area a pleasant place in which to live. The idea of building a balcony was an excellent idea as neighbours could speak to each other and watch children playing in the courtyard below. The neighbours were friendly and helpful especially when a serviceman came home on leave they would offer some of the rations to help out.

There was a parade of local shops in Kingsmead Way consisting of a greengrocers, grocers, Dr Saville's surgery, and the London County Council rent office. A caretaker lived locally but we never saw a Policeman.

A shelter was available for residents to go to during bombing raids although my mother refused to go down there preferring to play the piano and with neighbours joining in sang songs to defy Hitler. My brother Dennis was in the Air Force and I was a local Red Cross nurse. My other siblings were too young to be called up for service. Having failed my medical I was in a reserved occupation making cigarettes.

On September 7th 1940 at 5.30 pm the sirens started and the Battle of Britain began, I remember this vividly as my friend Dorothy and I was crossing the marshes when the sirens started. We told children to run home and we helped the younger ones, so the war really began.

As a Red Cross nurse I went to each block of flats asking for a contribution towards having a first aid flat in each block, no one refused. This was a time of great anxiety for our Jewish neighbours thinking that Hitler might invade and they would be sent to a concentration camp. The fact that we had Jewish neighbours was not an issue they were friendly people, we went to their sons Bar Mitzvah and Jewish weddings. We were all neighbours, class, colour or creed was not an issue. After the war our Jewish neighbours emigrated to South Africa and we are still in contact.

Each large flat had a one bedroom flat next door. We helped one elderly resident in the next door flat, by doing her shopping, and as the lady was deaf my brother fixed up a light in her room so that we let her know when the raids were on. My sister Joyce still keeps in touch with local residents.

Shopping was either in Marsh Hill, Chatsworth Road or Ridley Road. Rationing was difficult but we managed by having two allotments and growing our own veg.

My younger members of the family went to Pedro Youth Club and the Girl Guide Company that used the premises. Lady Rachel Bowes-Lyon was said to have visited this club on occasions. I continued to travel to Haggerston to attend the Methodist Church, which was my second home.

The Kingsmead Estate was never bombed but had blast from nearby raids and from the unexploded bombs being let off on the marshes. At one point an unexploded bomb was at St Paul's

Cathedral and they had fifteen minutes to get to the marshes, clearing all roads did this.

For me as a nurse I was out at all hours whenever a raid was nearby. At one session I was a few streets away in a hall when I ran out of first aid and asked the ARP to ask my sister to bring another box to me. She came round and saw the injured and fainted then was put in the ambulance with the more serious ones! Eventually I was asked by the Dalston Red Cross Commandant, Mr Nash, to go on secret war work, this I did and only recently divulged where I was. This was away from the flats getting the USA, Canadian and the Free Forces of Europe settled for embarkation, which became the D.Day landings. Recently I was interviewed by the BBC for a D.Day programme.

With the end of the war we had a Victory Party although rationing was still on we managed. After the war the estate was still a good place to live. We never had a Tenants Association but a Community Association, it was lively and tried to improve the estate. I remember a Mr Ward who was very good and hard working man, he and others felt the estate was worth giving time and energy to continue to improve it. I felt a great need was for a library and I wrote to the Hackney Council and a branch library was built on the estate.

People were very working class. You see them going off to work. A lot of the women were home with their families. I don't remember seeing many women out to work at the time because when the men came home everyone was offering a bit of something to help them out with rations. Very much working class and very much working class culture, by that I mean that you all had the same thing. You could leave your door open.

On looking back people were so friendly. People would wave, people would speak and gradually you got to know people from other blocks because the younger children you got to know them. I always felt a sense of harmony there. When the war ended people gradually moved out of the estate. My mother moved out in 1963.

It was a happy part of my life and I was saddened to read how it became one of the worst estates in England. I went back about eight years ago. We just drove round the streets and it looked ok to me but I just felt that it didn't look as being kept as nice as before, that was the feeling. I feel sure with the effort of the tenants and organisations on the estate it can regain its former success.

Brian Cook

Brian was born in 1949 and lived on the estate until he was a teenage into the late 1960s. He recalls the sense of community that existed. A Spurs supporter who spent some time in the army he still visits the estate periodically from his home in Holloway, North London.

I used to go to the Kingsmead School up the road there and Daubeney, and when I was eleven I went to South Hackney. I went past the Kingsmead School about four or five months ago and it has changed a little bit.

On a Saturday I used to go to Hackney Marshes, I used to play football and I don't know if they still do, we used to go round cleaning the cars for extra pocket money. There were pre-fabs right on the edge of Hackney Marshes opposite the flats, they went from one end to the other. They were so small.

The flats weren't nothing like they are now. In them days you could keep your doors open, you go in your neighbour's and they come in yours, leave the key on a bit of string behind the door and that was it, but now you can't.

That was in the 60's when I was living there, just leave our doors open, the neighbours come into your house, well they would knock on the door first and come in and we did the same.

At first we lived on Templemead, the top floor, number seventy four, and when me Mum was pregnant with me brother, my step-brother, we moved down to Runnymead on the first floor, number eighteen. Because of my Mum being pregnant and because there was no lifts in the flats, she had to walk up the stairs, so we were put in Runnymead.

It has not changed much, I remember the chip shop, is still there. The sweet shop I came past, and the doctors, that is where I had my doctors, just up the road there, but the flats have changed a lot, been redone and that.

The Golden Shoe Pub was still open the time before I came here, it was about five or six years ago because I went in there to see if I could see some old faces. I came down a few months back and it was closed down. I was looking round to see if I could see any of my old mates, all gone, I think they all moved out.

The best things about living on the estate was just playing in the grounds, the flats, going over the park, swings, I don't know if they are still there now, near Kingsmead School, we used to go over the marshes there and play football.

We used to get in trouble when we were small. We used to tie cotton from one letterbox, go on the other side of the flats tie string on one of the other doors, knock on that door and when they opened it the thing knocks on the other end and we laughed. We used to knock on the doors and run away like kids did in them days.

Everyone knew everyone. As you walked out on your street they would turn round and see you and say "Hello Brian", everyone knew everyone.

People wanted to move in there and when I left I found out people couldn't move out. When I moved it was the time when it was just changing. It was rough.

I am surprised the flats are still up because when I was there they were about sixty or seventy years old then, so I am surprised they are still up. They are doing work on them so that must have a bit of a future because if they were going to knock them down it would have been a waste of time to do all that work they are doing, it must have cost thousands.

If I didn't know anything about it, never seen the kids on the estate, I would have thought well all this work is going on, it must be good, I will probably move in.

Ewan McGregor

Born in Crieff, Perthshire, Scotland in 1971 the international film star Ewan McGregor has appeared in more than thirty films including Trainspotting and Star Wars, His most recent films include Moulin Rouge,Young Adam, Big Fish, and The Island. He lives in London with his wife and two daughters.

I lived on the estate for eight months. I can't remember the row; it's on the east side of the estate. We rented from an existing tenant. We got it out of the back of Loot. It was cheap and a good sized flat. It was economic. Before I lived in the Barbican and Manor Park.

There were smelly stairwells and scary pubs. It was difficult to get on public transport. We had some good times. I kept myself to myself.

I saw some guys crash a car into a wall, get out, laugh like fuck then run away. People thought of the estate as very rough.

8. How the project was carried out

The project was undertaken jointly by the Hackney Marsh Partnership, a voluntary agency based at the Kabin Project on the Kingsmead Estate and the University of Hertfordshire's Centre for Community Research. Funding for the project was obtained from Renaisi, the Hackney Wick SRB Partnership, from their Community Chest Programme.

From the outset of the project a steering group was set up to plan, monitor and oversee the project. Comprising of a number of residents, the Kingsmead Kabin's community worker, and researchers from the University of Hertfordshire, the group met regularly at the Kabin.

Resident's stories were gathered using tape recorded semi-structured interviews with existing and past residents. The criteria for selecting interviewees was individuals who were interested in 'talking about' their lives on the estate. In addition a number of resident's loaned the project photographs, and other personal memorabilia.

The steering group members who undertook interviews received training from the University researchers.

All the interviews were edited to maintain their flow and continuity and to preserve their spontaneity and recall of past events. In addition to ensure both factual and historical accuracy. This was with the agreement of the contributors. Edited transcripts were returned to the interviewees for approval and amendment.

The project was advertised widely across the estate using leaflets distributed to every household, and posters placed on estate buildings and community notice boards. Also the local newspaper, the Hackney Gazette, printed a request in its letter column for ex-residents to contact the project and ran a full page spread about the project.

9. Some References

Barwick S. (1991) Still a Slum. Spectator, May 11th.

Campbell D. (1996) Kingsmead Estate. Radio 5 Crime Desk, June 29th.

Cattell V. and Evans M. (1999) Neighbourhood Images in East London: Social capital and social networks on two East London estates. Joseph Rowntree Foundation.

Caunce S. (1994) Oral History and the Local Historian. Longman.

Christensen P. and O'Brien M. (Eds) (2002) Children in the City: Home Neighbourhood and Community (The Future of Childhood). Falmer Press.

Clifford D. (1995) Methods in Oral History and Social Work. Oral History, Autumn.

Holman B. (1981) Kids at the Door. Blackwell.

Holman B. (1998) Faith in the Poor. Lion Publishing.

Huerta and Flemmer (2001) Latina Women Speak – Using Oral History. Social Education 65(5), pp.279-277.

Guardian (1993) E. Pearce, Hackney's terror estate finding a civil cure.

Green R. (1997) Community Action Against Poverty. A Poverty Profile of the Kingsmead Estate in Hackney. Kingsmead Kabin.

Martin R. (1995) Oral History in Social Work, Research, Assessment and Intervention. Sage.

Murphy J. and Fearon M. (1985) Devil's Island. Marshalls.

Pearce E. (1993) Hackney's terror estate finding a civil cure. Guardian, June 12th.

News Chronicle (1939) Bottle of Beer for the King, News Chronicle. March 31st, 1939.

Rivera F. and Erlich J. (1992) Community Organising in a Diverse Society. Allyn and Bacon.

Toynbee P. (2003) Hard Work. Life in Low Pay Britain. Bloomsbury Publishing.

Ward. C. (1974) Tenants take over. London: Architectural Press.

Ward C. (1978) The Child in the City. Colin Ward. London: Architectural Press.

10. Author Biography

Dr Roger Green was born in Walthamstow, East London. He is Director of the Centre for Community Research, School of Social, Community and Health Studies, at the University of Hertfordshire in Hatfield. A regular contributor to academic and community publications he continues to undertake participatory action research with residents of the Kingsmead Estate.

Printed in the United Kingdom
by Lightning Source UK Ltd.
107579UKS00001B/115-207

9 781845 490720